HAUNTED UTICA

HAUNTED UTICA

MOHAWK VALLEY GHOSTS
AND OTHER HISTORIC HAUNTS

DENNIS WEBSTER AND BERNADETTE PECK

Haunted America

Published by Haunted America
A Division of The History Press
Charleston, SC 29403
www.historypress.net

First published 2014

Manufactured in the United States

ISBN 978.1.62619.138.9

Library of Congress CIP data applied for.

This tome is dedicated to all the ghost hunters and enthusiasts chasing down the unexplained and seeking to complete the journey of lost souls, or the *gwi* (prounounced "gway"), as spirits are called in China. We are all searching for answers in this life, and if not… perhaps the next.

—Dennis

This book is dedicated to the ones who wish to travel down many paths, all convening on a very mysterious world of the unknown. So when least expected, supernatural things can happen.

—Bernadette

CONTENTS

PREFACE

As I have ventured forth on additional hunts of the paranormal kind with the Ghost Seekers of Central New York, I have finally come to understand my addiction to the spiritual safari. I have concluded that the reason I love ghost seeking so much is the need to find answers, the quest for connection and the wanting for curiosity. These are all flames to my mental moth. I have witnessed, smelled and heard things I cannot explain, and for those out there who are skeptical of these accounts, I respect you and your view of the paranormal. Most of us carbon stalks need to know things exist through mortal interaction, yet faith has us believe in angels and gods. If you, dear reader, ever have a chance to go along for a spiritual investigation, I encourage you to do so, with an open mind and heart, and you might just have communication with a ghost. I respect the craft of ghost hunting and admire greatly the Ghost Seekers of Central New York for the group members perform their investigations with civility, respect and passion. I'm grateful for them counting me among their team members. Now please, enjoy the tales, and know that these are told without embellishment and are 100 percent true. These paranormal interactions occurred under the watchful eyes, ears and nose right down to my left hand that scribes on a pad of paper—under flashlight at midnight, of course.

—Dennis

I believe myself to be somewhat of a detective, pursuing ghosts in a very deliberate manner. Much of the time is spent sitting around waiting for something to happen, and yet, we continue to do it, week after week, year after year. Why? It's all very intriguing and my greatest fascination. Regardless of how it all started, through investigating tales and haunted places, I have found there is nothing like hearing a really good story and taking a trip to visit a graveyard or a reportedly haunted house. Most important in a paranormal investigation, there must be a purpose. Why would a place be haunted and what is the history of the location? Why is the phenomenon happening? These are the questions my team members and I seek to answer. We still have much to learn when it comes to the supernatural. This is why we have become detectives, and with that, a book such as this plays a very important part.

—Bernadette

ACKNOWLEDGEMENTS

I wish to thank my co-writer and lead investigator/founder of the Ghost Seekers of Central New York, Bernadette Peck. I would like to send great appreciation to the rest of the Ghost Seekers of Central New York: Josh Aust, Len Bragg, Helen Clausen, Irene Crewell, "Paranormal" Ed Livingston, Joe Ostrander, Carol Pearo and David Peck. Thank you to George Abel, Michael Bosak, Kevin Brown, Judi Cusworth, Darlene DeSiato, Tony DeSiato, Kathy Durr, Nichole Grant, Brian Howard, Jerry Kraus, Amy Lamberto, Marlene Marello, Erin Murphy, Jim Murphy, Eric Newman, Renee Reile, Carl Saporito, Gary Seelman, Rob Seelman, Vince Scalise, Alan Smith, Debbie Smith, Brian Waterman, Gerard Waterman and the Oneida County Historical Society. Thank you to the gracious hosts of the investigations included in this book: Durhamville Fire Department, First Presbyterian Church of Utica, Forest Hill Cemetery, Henry Hiteman Engine & Fire Hose Company, Landmark Society of Greater Utica, Madison House, Newport Masonic Temple, Oneida County Historical Society, Players of Utica, Stanley Center for the Arts and the Vernon Public Library. A big thank-you goes out to my wife, Kelly, and my children for their support of my adventures. Thank you to my mother and father, brothers and sisters, friends and supporters. I love you all! A thank-you to Whitney Landis and the entire staff at The History Press for giving these tales a home. Finally, a thank-you to Evelyn Webster for always being there to read my words and providing feedback and encouragement.

—Dennis

Again, I thank my writing buddy Dennis Webster and the team I could not do without. A special thanks to all the involved parties in these investigations for their honesty and graciousness in allowing our investigations to take place.

—Bernadette

GHOST SEEKERS OF CENTRAL NEW YORK

The Ghost Seekers of Central New York have been conducting paranormal research for well over a decade, with hundreds of locations investigated, documented, debunked, revealed and archived. These investigations are not for the faint of heart and are 100 percent true. We walk dusty basements at midnight searching for confirmation from the realm of the dead. In these ghost hunts, we always deploy the most advanced equipment and go by the proper protocols and ethics of the highest order, but nothing can replace eyes, ears, nose and mind. Our current lineup of members includes: lead investigator/founder Bernadette Peck, Len Bragg, "Paranormal" Ed Livingston, David Peck, psychic Irene Crewell, Dennis Webster, Josh Aust, Joe Ostrander, Helen Clausen and Carol Pearo. Although all these tales are true, some names had to be changed to protect those who wish to remain unknown. Names of people have been changed upon request or to protect their identities. These people are identified within this book with an asterisk (*).

GEAR WE USE

The gear that's used in the field that you'll read about in this book includes digital recorders for gathering electronic voice phenomenon (EVP); K2 and Gauss meter for measuring electromagnetism; a spirit box, which searches radio frequencies and reroutes words to a speaker; digital cameras; hardwired

Ghost Seekers of Central New York.

night-vision video cameras; and hand-held night-vision video cameras. We use all the protocols and ethics of proper ghost hunting and debunk any questionable evidence.

PSYCHIC DISCLAIMER

The Ghost Seekers of Central New York utilize both psychics and mediums on investigations. While no investigative tool is considered to be 100 percent accurate, our use of these individuals is as investigative tools. Our psychics and mediums identify areas of an investigation site that may be conducive to higher levels of paranormal activity, as well as openly participate during an investigation, adding what they are sensing at the time. Information obtained from our psychics and mediums is carefully reviewed, as is all our evidence, and when corroborated, it is included in our findings to our clients.

—Irene Crewell
paranormal investigator
with the Ghost Seekers and world-class psychic

UTICA

Chapter 1

THE HISTORY OF UTICA

The city of Utica is centrally located in New York State and lies next to the New York State Thruway between Syracuse and Albany. Utica sits in the geological region that many refer to as the Mohawk Valley. Utica is a city long revered for its embrace of immigrants and refugees from around the world who have flooded the area with the sounds, tastes and colors of many cultures. Utica, oddly enough, was not the original name of this community nestled on the banks of the Mohawk River. The Iroquois were the original inhabitants of the area, with the Mohawk Valley mainly occupied by member tribes the Mohawk and Oneida Indians. The Iroquois have many legends, but Utica being haunted goes back to the legend of Oniate, also known as "Dry Fingers." This vengeful spirit consisted of a disembodied mummified hand and arm that would punish with afflictions those who behaved badly. Perhaps Oniate is still around today moving from home to home in Utica.

The Mohawk Valley and Utica were first settled in the late eighteenth century by the Europeans who built Fort Schuyler, named after Colonel Phillip Schuyler, a hero in the French and Indian War. The fort would eventually dissolve, but the area would adopt the name Old Fort Schuyler. This would be the name for years until local men gathered in Baggs Tavern to decide on a new name for the village. Names were written on slips of paper with every man present scribing his wish for the new name. It was Erastus Clark who wrote down the name Utica, an ancient port city in Carthage that was the first colony to be founded by the Phoenicians in North Africa.

The name Utica was incorporated in 1798 and stands to this day. Utica would thrive and grow on the backs of Italian, Welsh, German, Polish and Irish immigrants who would labor in textile factories that blossomed along the Mohawk River. Utica Sheets, one such company, was known worldwide for its top-quality textiles. Utica's population swelled in the early to mid-twentieth century and hosted expansion into manufacturing that enjoyed the central location and access to the Barge Canal, the Mohawk River and, post World War II, the New York State Thruway. Utica would decrease in population in the latter part of the twentieth century as jobs were lost and industry moved to other countries. However, the late twentieth and early twenty-first centuries proved a boost to the area, with new refugee populations from Bosnia, Somalia and other countries. Utica today is known as a city that loves and embraces people, religions, cultures and colors from around the globe. The city hosts hundreds of grand estates, structures and buildings that are awe-inspiring and hand-built with top craftsmanship. It's these grand old places that host ghosts and spirits in the night.

Chapter 2

FOREST HILL CEMETERY

Utica, New York—August 3, 2013

The Forest Hill Cemetery sits atop a hill on the edge of the city of Utica and hosts the last resting place of many of the power brokers, politicians and founders with lasting legacies from the past couple hundred years in history. Forest Hill Cemetery has over fifty thousand people buried and continues to add to that number, as it is still very active.

The first thing you see when you approach Forest Hill is the Gothic stone main entrance that is unlike that of any cemetery you will ever see. Inside are buried people from kings of industry and powerful politicians to orphans and lunatics from the Utica Asylum. Just a taste of some of the historic graves:

- At one time, Roscoe Conkling (1829–1888) was considered one of the most powerful men in the United States. He was mayor of Utica, Oneida County district attorney and United States senator and was asked numerous times to sit on the Supreme Court.
- Samuel Beardsley (1856–1932) participated in the War of 1812, was the Oneida County district attorney and served as a United States congressman, New York State attorney general and chief justice of the New York State Supreme Court.
- John Butterfield (1801–1869) ran the company Butterfield, Wasson & Company that would go on to be American Express. He was instrumental in the early stages of telegraph communication. His son Daniel was a general for the Union during the Civil War, was

Gothic entrance to Forest Hill Cemetery.

awarded the Congressional Medal of Honor and composed the military tune taps.

- Ellis Roberts (1827–1918) was editor of the *Utica Morning Herald* and a member of the United States House of Representatives. He was assistant United States treasurer and then became treasurer of the United States when he was appointed by President William McKinley.

There are also dozens and dozens more people of distinction buried in the hallowed historic grounds of the Forest Hill Cemetery.

It would prove difficult for the Ghost Seekers to decide what graves to visit in the night. We would have to follow Bernadette's psychic intuition, Gerard's vast knowledge and Tony's favorites. The trio did not disappoint on their guidance, and we experienced a magical paranormal evening in a place of overflowing history and tragedy. It's the human condition we all live every day.

The night began with a meeting in the office of Gerard Waterman, superintendant of Forest Hill. His elegant office is attached to the Gothic stone entrance and is adorned with handcrafted furniture that represents a history all its own. The Ghost Seekers of Central New

York was represented by lead investigator and founder Bernadette Peck; her husband and crackerjack paranormal investigator, David Peck; and paranormal investigators Helen Clausen and Dennis Webster. We were thrilled that we would be given the honor of being the first ever ghost-hunting group to be able to investigate Forest Hill after dark. The caretaker locked the doors as the sun fell over the western rim of the Earth. We talked with Gerard and his son Brian Waterman, who would be along for the investigation. We would have the husband-wife team of Tony and Darlene Desiato as our tour guides. The group had handpicked several of the most interesting grave sites in the hope that their beauty would be a conduit for activity.

It was a balmy summer night with no wind or rain in the forecast—a perfect night to troll a cemetery for the personalities of the dead. Before we could start, we needed the sun to fall completely over the edge of the earth to envelope Forest Hill in delightful darkness. We went into the meeting room adjacent to Gerard's office, where the Ghost Seekers of

Entrance to the Forest Hill Cemetery around 1900. *Courtesy of the Library of Congress.*

Central New York was given the special privilege of looking through the interment logs, which are the records of the dead and buried from 1849 through the modern age. We marveled at the overstuffed volumes that had been handwritten in beautiful quill ink that one never sees today. It was interesting to see the names, ages at death, causes of demise and the plots in which they are buried. Reasons of death were listed as exhaustion, unknown, consumption, insanity and dozens of others. The saddest part was reading about the young children, especially the ones who had come from the House of the Good Sheppard or had been orphans. Gerard told us that Forest Hill has a massive amount of people buried on its grounds and continues to add new residents.

We asked Gerard and his son Brian if they had any ghost stories or if any possible paranormal incidents had happened at Forest Hill. They told us of the man who was walking his pair of beagles on the dirt road up by plots 12 and 13, by the chapel, when he saw two young boys dressed in nineteenth-century clothing. They were clearly ghosts, as the man stated that he could see through them. The boys ran into the woods and evaporated. We could only hope the spirits would come alive to greet us. Even when there is reported haunted activity, we can never expect or guarantee anything happening on an investigation. All we can do is hunt for the paranormal game.

We started out with an opening prayer to bring forth friendly spirits and discourage any dark entities from interloping in our sphere. Little did we know that we would get a paranormal rarity within the first few minutes. As the group was walking up the main drive, we were all talking. We had our digital recorders on for the entire spiritual hunt in case we might capture something on our travels. We also had our K2 meters to monitor electromagnetic activity, as well as digital cameras and a night-vision digital video camera that was being operated by David.

We were only a few hundred yards up the road when we all noticed that David had stayed back and was pointing his camera at the grove of trees lining the road. We waited while Bernadette walked down alone to join her husband. I had a feeling something was happening, as they stayed there for a few minutes. When they rejoined all of us, we received a shock. David had been filming the trees. In the squid-ink dark, our human eyes do not have the rods and cones that allow us clear view, but a night-vision camera makes things clear. David had been filming the woods and captured the ghost of a young woman dressed in late nineteenth-century clothing peering at him from behind one of the trees. He froze. He took a step to the right to try to get her completely. She moved when he did, as if she were playing some kind

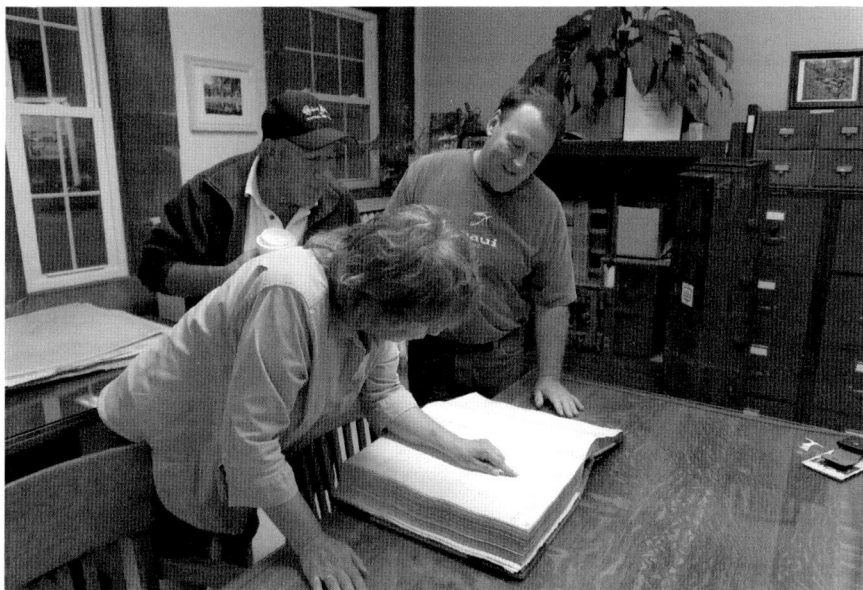

Interment records reviewed by Forest Hill superintendent Gerard Waterman and paranormal investigators Bernadette and David Peck.

of paranormal hide-and-seek. This was incredible. Bernadette was floored, as she says David, who had been on hundreds of investigations over a multi-decade career of ghost hunting, rarely has this type of event. We all paused. It was a rare occurrence. When this was happening with David, I had taken a photo of the same woods but farther up, and I picked up a couple spirit lights and orbs in between some trees.

We walked all the way up to our first spot, next to a beautiful headstone that had a carved stone anchor on the top. Out of the respect for the living relatives, we have decided not to mention specific graves or names of locations where we did our electronic voice phenomenon (EVP) or the exact headstone where evidence was found. I will make one exception to this rule at the grave of the consort—or, as they would use in our modern vernacular, mistress—since that marker has only a first name. Anyhow, we marveled at the splendor and serenity of the cemetery at night. Helen was getting photos with orbs, and Bernadette picked up ghostly voices in between a few of the large mausoleums. The digital recorder did a good job since the night had no wind or noise. We came upon a grove of little square stones flat in the ground with a tall obelisk in the center. Gerard told us this was the tribute

Right: Resurrection woman headstone at Forest Hill Cemetery.

Below: Paranormal investigators Helen Clausem and Bernadette Peck examine a headstone.

and the burial place of the orphans. It was sad to read the names and life dates of these precious angels. There was one-year-old Nora, seven-year-old Elizabeth and eight-year-old Emma, among dozens of others.

As mentioned earlier, we got an interesting interaction at the grave site of Margaret the consort. The term "consort" refers to a lady-in-waiting, a companion, a geisha or a high-priced friend with benefits but with a nineteenth-century title. This flat stone was off in a corner near some trees, but the entire group was drawn to it. We stood next to the grave of the consort and asked questions about being a prostitute and whether she was sad to be off alone with only her first name on her marker. I made a joke about her profession, and Bernadette chimed in with a colorful metaphor. At that moment, the wind picked up and the trees bent toward us in the dark. This would not happen the rest of the night. It was random, and it was spooky. As we were all walking away, Helen, Bernadette and I all heard the voice of a young woman. I could not make out the words, but it was enough to cause me to spin around, as did the ladies, and marvel at what we had just heard. We were all in agreement that Margaret was not pleased with our descriptions of her. We apologized for the offense and sallied forth.

As we walked from grave to grave, Tony and Gerard discussed the history of the most famous occupants. We put Darlene to work and gave her the K2 ghost meter to carry, but it was not picking up any activity. I was able to get a photo of Helen and Tony that showed a spirit light right above their heads. A couple hours into the investigation, two amazing paranormal events happened. Everyone had decided to stop and take a break when Tony suddenly witnessed a ball of light slaloming through the trees on the backside of the cemetery. We were on the highest hill, far in the back, near the oldest gravestones at Forest Hill. This ball of light had to be intelligent, as it moved up, down and around the trees and then faded out of our plane of existence.

The other event involved Helen, Bernadette and me. We were sitting on the steps of one ornate grave site that I will describe as that of an illustrious man with impeccable credentials. The other group members were far across the road looking at other headstones, and it was just the three of us sitting there. All you could hear were the crickets singing and the frogs of the lily-pad pond croaking their midnight serenade. I was quiet as Helen and Bernadette discussed how marvelous and beautiful this grave site was and how a cup of coffee would make the moment perfect. I had left my digital recorder on during this conversation. At the time, the ladies and I heard nothing, yet upon playback, there was a soft but clear whisper asking, "What the hell?" The only thing I can surmise is that the gentleman buried beneath our feet did not take kindly to idle chatter about hot beverages. He was a man, when alive, who certainly would not allow any tomfoolery in his vicinity. It's rare to get a lengthy and totally clear EVP, especially outdoors, where there tend to be environmental noises interfering. As soon as this exchange about coffee finished, Darlene walked over and said she felt a chill. Brian was very respectful and quiet yet once in a while asked paranormal questions. There is no doubt he was interested in what was occurring.

On the way back down the hill, we stopped at a large Celtic cross. I had never beheld something so grand and ornate. It was tall and looming in the night, with carved swirls, and it was circled on the ground by small hand-carved gravestones that resembled battle shields. The next stop was at the mass burial site of the young schoolteachers who had been killed in a train crash in New Jersey over a century ago. The young teachers between the ages of eighteen and twenty had been going to a conference when the accident happened. The site was now a place where what was left of the ladies had been buried together. They were smart young ladies snuffed from this world on the eve of their lives.

One the way back down the hill, close to the end of our expedition, Bernadette stopped at the graves of the children who had passed from the House of the Good Sheppard. These gravestones were small and many in number, with most of those buried there under the age of ten. Back in the nineteenth century, children passed away from many ailments we have cures for today. Bernadette said a soft prayer as she waltzed through the stones.

We arrived back at Gerard's office by the Gothic stone archway. We held hands and offered a closing prayer to keep any of us from carrying out spirits. We felt honored and privileged that Gerard had allowed the Ghost Seekers to walk hallowed and sacred ground. After this experience, Tony and Darlene were no longer ghost-hunting virgins, and Brian had something to talk about with his grass-cutting buddies. All in all, it was a very successful and thrilling investigation at one of the most grand and historic cemeteries in the United States.

ADDITIONAL OBSERVATIONS FROM BERNADETTE PECK

Having the ability to walk the hallowed ground of the Forest Hill Cemetery at night was a privilege, and the spirits did not disappoint, with some exceptional paranormal interaction that resulted in some great evidence.

Celtic cross at Forest Hill Cemetery.

The mourning lady headstone at Forest Hill Cemetery.

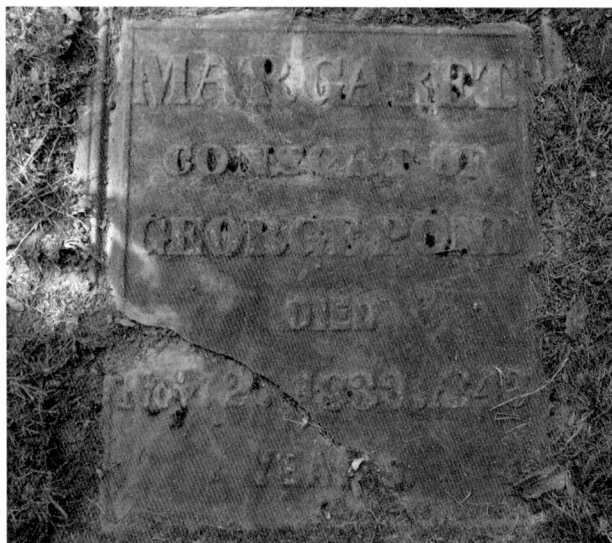

Grave of Margaret the consort.

Gerard Waterman was kind enough to escort us, and we had special guides in Tony and Darlene DeSiato. I was honored to be able to visit with Gerard in his office and be able to skim through the interment records of people who had been buried over one hundred years ago. Some of the reasons listed for death ranged from consumption and insanity to drowning and the flu. Skimming my fingers across the pages, I felt the sadness of thousands of departed souls. Conducting the investigation was difficult, with background noise interfering with the digital recorders, but we were still able to capture the voices of those who are dead. As we were walking up the main drive to get to the first set of historic graves, David picked up on his hand-held night-vision camera a young female spirit adorned in a white dress peeking at him from around the trees. While the rest of the group moved on, Dave hung back, as if he were psychically drawn to the lonely little girl ghost. Although she revealed herself to David, he stayed frozen and didn't move closer, as he felt she did not want him getting any nearer. Dennis and Helen also picked up some spirit lights on their cameras at the same time. We all halted, and I walked back to David. I'm not used to seeing my husband in this kind of trance. The little girl in white had chosen him to witness her apparition, and she dissipated when I got near.

Within minutes of this ghostly appearance, we approached a mausoleum where Helen witnessed a misty light in white. Right after this, we started to have equipment failures, and batteries drained. This is a common paranormal occurrence. We stopped at a historic grave that had a large stone anchor on the top, and right away, I heard voices coming from the woods. It was impossible that they came from any human, as Gerard had locked the front gates and we were the only carbon stalks alive on two feet. It was clearly the voices of the deceased calling out to us from the moonlit trees. The others had several ghostly interactions including a few fantastic EVPs. I'm hoping we get the opportunity to return to the historic and haunted Forest Hill Cemetery.

Chapter 3

UTICA PSYCHIATRIC HOSPITAL "OLD MAIN"

Utica, New York—November 16, 2013

The evening was unseasonably warm and the lunar phase close to full, so the Ghost Seekers decided to take a paranormal fieldtrip to what many considered the most haunted building in the city of Utica. The Utica psychiatric hospital has long been the Holy Grail of haunted sites, not only in the Utica area but also nationally. It was on this balmy fall evening that a one-hour tour provided frights, thrills, sadness and, most importantly, clear-cut evidence of a haunting, the kind of evidence that would amaze even the most seasoned ghost hunter.

When you drive through the heart of West Utica, the sight of what many call "Old Main" looms out like a menacing gray columned beast. Old Main is the largest building on the grounds of the Utica psychiatric hospital. The ominous gray monolith is fronted by large columns that, as one approaches, look like an evil grinning face with massive stone teeth.

Old Main was built in 1843 in the Greek Revival style of architecture. It was the first mental institution of its kind in New York State and one of the first nationally. The original name of the facility was the State Lunatic Asylum at Utica. The original director of the facility was Dr. Amariah Brigham, who was a pioneer in the treatment and diagnosis of those who were mentally ill. He even founded a print shop where he published the *American Journal of Insanity* and also printed writings by the patients in a periodical called the *Opal*. Dr. Brigham was also the inventor of the Utica Crib, a device that attempted to hold and calm a patient instead of chaining

Old Main opened in 1843. *Courtesy Jeff Berman.*

him or her to a wall. The patient would lie down in the crib, which had a locked cover. The device resembled a birdcage, except that the patient was forced to lie on his back and could not sit up, roll over or get out. In our age, the device looks like a medieval torture mechanism, yet at the time, it received accolades and use in asylums nationwide. The Utica Crib was constructed of wood and sometimes iron, and patients could spend years locked inside, like one patient who was documented to have spent over a decade inside the crib. The Utica Crib stopped being used at the State Lunatic Asylum in Utica in 1887.

In 1978, Old Main had its last patients transferred to other buildings and was closed to patient care forever. In 2004, a portion of the first floor was opened as a records archive and a repository for the New York State Office of Mental Health. It was on these most sacred grounds that we respectfully reached out to the sad and lonely ghosts trapped walking the empty halls of this noble structure. The investigation would have to be constrained to the exterior, as Old Main now has a fence, topped with barbed wire to keep the curious at bay, encircling the entire structure.

Artist's rendering of the 1843 State Lunatic Asylum at Utica, or Old Main, as it is known in modern times. *Courtesy Dennis Webster.*

The grand columns of Old Main.

Form 126–Adm.

State of New York—Utica State Hospital

Permission is granted

to be absent from the Hospital
until 12 P.m. Date Dec. 24
Returned m.

Nightwatch

Left: A patient's Christmas Eve pass from 1880. *Courtesy Dennis Webster.*

Below: The architect of Old Main, William Clarke, designed it in the Greek Revival style.

The fencing also has warning signs posted that any trespassers will be arrested and prosecuted to the full extent of the law. The Ghost Seekers of Central New York always show respect to the law and only tread on grounds that are approved. We would not violate the signs, but you could feel the pull of the spirits when you stepped up to the fence and looked up at the windows that long-ago mental patients fogged with their breaths. The group had tried every legal means necessary to gain inside access but was denied. With the age of the building and the fragility of the structure, one can only surmise that this was the reason, but perhaps it is also a fear of the ghosts of long-dead patients speaking up for their spiritual rights.

We had only about half of our normal team, but the night investigators included our lead investigator and founder Bernadette Peck; her solid-as-rock husband, David Peck; psychic Irene Crewell; Josh Aust; and paranormal investigator and writer Dennis Webster, who would be scribing the proceedings for this book. We would be going with one night-vision video camera that David would be operating, a couple digital recorders, a K2 meter and a digital camera. The first thing we did was gather and say a prayer to the lost souls of the asylum and also ask St. David and St. Michael to protect us from the evils of the netherworld. Bernadette always leads us in the prayer. We always hold hands in a circle, close our eyes and bow our heads, not only out of respect but also out of fear of anything dark attaching itself to us and hitching a ride home. We gathered our gear and headed off.

As we walked along the fence, we spoke of the outdated methods of patient care that were not unusual in the past. Chains, confinement, restraint and the Utica Crib were all standard operating procedure. We talked of the movie *One Flew Over the Cuckoo's Nest*, which portrayed the inner workings of an insane asylum. We all discussed the feelings of sadness coming from the looming gloomy structure. I was snapping a bunch of digital pictures with nothing being seen. David was shooting night-vision video of the patient windows. I felt a flatness in the air, but that was about to change as we walked around to the back. We were along the back fence, walking on the grass with crunching leaves beneath our feet, when Bernadette heard the distinct sound of a woman humming. "Hhhmmm…mmmmmm…mmmmm" went the sound, and it was not made by any of the investigators. We halted and stayed in the spot for some time while Irene began to feel overwhelmed by the sadness of the ghost patients walking the grounds. She was so overcome that she did something I never thought I'd see: she cried. Tears streamed down her cheeks, and we were all stunned, as Irene is normally rock solid and a very seasoned investigator and communicator with the dead. Josh heard a scream that, sadly, was not recorded.

It was at this time that we all became a little nervous as we watched a roaming pack of large dogs come between a couple of the outbuildings. They stopped and stared at us. I got the feeling they were evil guardians, hellhounds, roaming the psych center grounds to keep the good at bay. It was odd. It's hard to describe the pure evil that emanated from that pack—and we are all animal lovers and dog owners. They finally moved on, and Bernadette lit a cigarette. We were talking about how in the old days, cigarettes were used as a reward system for good behavior and probably one of the few pleasures the mental patients had. Bernadette said

Visitors to the asylum. Old Main was one of the top tourist destinations in the nineteenth century. *Courtesy of the Oneida County Historical Society.*

This postcard from 1905 depicts the lavish grounds and gardens designed by world-famous landscaper Andrew Jackson Downing. *Courtesy Dennis Webster.*

to the spirits, "Would you like a cigarette?" and clear as day on the digital recorder, we received a ghostly sigh. It was loud and distinct and in the tone of a ghost that desperately wanted a cigarette and missed smoking.

Irene felt the area possibly had a cemetery, and we wondered where all the patients had been buried in the nineteenth century. In our past investigation at Forest Hill Cemetery, we had seen the old interment records, and some ledger entries had mentioned Utica psychiatric patients having been buried in the cemetery after they died from "insanity." But these records represented only a few of the thousands who had been through the asylum over the century it had been open.

Bernadette and David mentioned seeing something moving inside when Irene stated, "This is a bad place." Josh agreed and mentioned he was seeing a middle-aged woman, with fair skin and dirty blond hair, who was very ugly. It was at this point that Bernadette received a paranormal bouquet in the scent of flowers. It was so strong that she could taste it in her mouth. She came up to each one of us to sniff our scents and knew what she had caught a whiff of was the perfume of a ghost coming into our plane of existence to tantalize her nostrils. Along with the flowery smell, Bernadette felt extreme pressure in her chest. I do not consider myself psychic, but I had a feeling of patients being exploited, a feeling of a gentle, fragile human being taken advantage of by caregivers. It was not a good feeling, and I was glad we moved on.

The group walked around the side of the building and was stunned by the porches. Creepy is the only way I can describe them. There were three stories of wire-enclosed windows. Josh claimed it looked like a haunted house and that you could see it as a large evil face. David stated it looked like something out of a movie. Josh, who is becoming a stronger psychic with each outing, saw people in agony. Irene wanted to go inside and release the tormented souls to the light but could only do her work for the ghosts brave enough to approach her for release. She was giving them freedom to roam in heaven, away from their earthbound spiritual torment.

It was at this time that I started getting spirit lights in front of the building. The strangest was a photo of something none of us had ever seen. It was a large, thick, paranormal ectoplasm streak that looked as if the spirit of a psychiatric patient was coming through a window and heading up into the sky. Right when I was getting these photos, Bernadette's K2 meter started to spike up to 2 and then up to 3. The theory is that proximity to a ghost will cause a spike in electromagnetism.

We put our equipment away, and I looked at my watch. We had only been there one hour, yet the strength and interaction with the ghosts was incredible and emotionally draining. We all felt weary from the investigation and were glad to say our closing prayer and leave the Utica psychiatric hospital, placing the cold columns of Old Main in our rearview mirrors. Sadly, the spirits of the insane will remain trapped behind those gray slab walls until a kindly person of authority gives our group permission to go in and cleanse the place.

A barbed-wired fence and "No Trespassing" signs keep the curious away from Old Main.

ADDITIONAL OBSERVATIONS FROM BERNADETTE PECK

The most amazing piece of evidence was to come after the investigation had concluded. I was going through the evidence with my husband, David, and there didn't seem to be anything of consequence when, suddenly, there it was. When David was filming the patient windows of the insane asylum, we captured on film the shadow figure of what looked like a man standing in one of the windows. The camera had stopped long enough to capture this ghost move away from the window. Capturing a ghost walking and moving on a digital camera is incredibly rare, yet there it was. We knew there was nobody in the building that night as we have a friend who has been inside the place and knows the schedule and movements of the maintenance crew. The building is unoccupied on Saturday nights. There were no cars in the parking lot but ours, and there was nothing but a pack of dogs roaming the grounds. Plus, you can see from the video that this is not a human form, as it is darker than coal and clearly a shadow entity. We brought the video to our ghost meeting, and the paranormal investigators who had been part of this investigation were stunned. It's one of the most incredible pieces of ghost evidence caught in my more than two decades of ghost seeking.

I found the hellhounds to be disturbing, and they sent a chill down my spine. We were in the back of the Old Main building when things went crazy paranormally, and I heard a woman humming. Irene became overwhelmed, and Josh was picking up spiritual visions of patients. At this time, I felt something odd, and I turned to see a pack of hounds staring at us. They were off in the distance, but I could feel the evil. Irene is a huge dog lover, and she was scared enough that she scrambled in her bag to locate pepper spray. The seconds seemed hours until the hounds of hell broke away and ran off between two other buildings on the psychiatric center grounds.

It's my greatest wish that we be granted inside access to complete an investigation. I know there are ghosts trapped inside Old Main that are lonely and wish to communicate, and Irene would be able to use her psychic ability to move them into the peace and grace of the light of the better plane.

Chapter 4

THE CHURCH HOUSE

Utica, New York—May 26, 2012, and September 15, 2012

The Church House on Genesee Street in Utica is now attached to and associated with the First Presbyterian Church, but it was originally built as a family residence. The home was built in the Georgian style according to the specifications laid out by Robert MacKinnon between 1890 and 1900. In 1898, the *Utica Observer* wrote an article describing the MacKinnon home and raved about the rooms, closets, chambers and the extravagant third-floor ballroom. The home was large, plush and declared to be among the most beautiful in Utica. MacKinnon was a cotton mill owner from Little Falls whose empire included several mills. Mr. MacKinnon was wealthy enough that he had a housekeeper, four maids, a gardener, two chauffeurs and a laundress. In addition, he lavished his children with annual allowances of $25,000 per year per child, which was an exorbitant sum for the early twentieth century.

At one time, Robert MacKinnon threw a party in honor of his young daughter Molly. It was a dance in the ballroom, and over seven hundred invitations went out all over New York State. The *Utica Daily Press* wrote an article raving about the decorations, food and noble guests.

When the MacKinnon family lived in the Church House, their daughter Molly met a young man who claimed he was a European count, and she announced that she had become engaged to be married to the count. The family was not happy and thought they had talked Molly out of going through with her wedding plans, but it was a ruse, as she eloped with the charming young nobleman. However, Molly soon discovered that the young man was not of European nobility, and not only was he not a count, but he was also still married, which sent Molly into a downward spiral. She ran away from Utica and was never heard from again.

Mr. MacKinnon eventually went broke when the textile market bottomed out. He ended up moving his family from their beloved mansion, which was purchased by the First Presbyterian Church right next door. Eventually, the church constructed a hallway in 1960 that joined the two buildings, but it is the Church House that continues to have many ghostly sightings. The MacKinnon family and others theorize that Molly ended up dying of a broken heart and believe her spirit has returned to her home in Utica, haunting it to this day. She was not an only child and left behind two sisters and two brothers, yet it is Molly who roams the plush rooms of the Church House.

Over many years, there have been numerous members of the First Presbyterian Church who have seen Molly. Most do not want to go on record, but there was at least one person who talked to the press about his ghostly interactions. In a story in the *Observer Dispatch*, reporter David

The Church House.

The staircase where the spirit of Molly MacKinnon has been spotted by numerous people.

Dudajek interviewed David Vosmus, who had a well-known interaction with the ghost of Molly MacKinnon. It was Easter morning in 1978 when Vosmus was in the Church House kitchen, where he was cooking sausage for breakfast at 3:00 a.m. He was all alone. He told Dudajek that he was sitting in the kitchen reading the newspaper, waiting for the sausage to cook, when the hair on his neck rose. Something made him look up, and he saw a woman with long hair standing in the doorway. He could see through the spirit, which didn't speak but just stared right at him for a lengthy seven seconds before it slowly dissipated. Vosmus had been described as a large, rough man who would not frighten easily, yet when other church members showed up, the man was white as a sheet.

Another story tells of an electrician who had been hired to install a fire alarm and had to stay alone in the building overnight. The man knew nothing of the haunted stories and ended up having a night of fright when an entity went straight through his body and sent shivers down his spine.

Another person who came forward with a story of interacting with Molly was Stan Wiatr. Stan was taking an item up to the third-floor storage area when he opened the door and saw Molly standing in the middle of the room. He quickly closed the door and fled.

The Ghost Seekers of Central New York did a paranormal presentation at the Oneida County Historical Society, which is right across the street from the Church House, and we talked with George Abel. George is a volunteer and runs the bookstore for the historical society. He is a church elder, caretaker and historian at the First Presbyterian Church. He talked to the group about the haunted history of the Church House and asked if we would like to conduct an investigation. Bernadette thought it would be a great opportunity to verify the stories and legends of this beautiful mansion. We showed up on a sunny Saturday evening on May 26, 2012, and George was there to greet us with a warm handshake and a smile. On this night, the team members were lead investigator, Bernadette; her husband, David; Kate*; Mike*; Ed; Len; and myself. George took us on a tour of the First Presbyterian Church and then the Church House. Both were large and beautiful structures that were connected by a block walkway. We were going to be doing our investigation only in the Church House, which was three stories and had a basement. The first room we saw was the first-floor dining room, or what I call the "blue room" because of the blue leather wallpaper. Next was the music room, which was done in a yellow tone and had the names of composers along the tops of the walls. The foyer and the stairwell to the second floor was the place George pointed out as having the most sightings of Molly. Bernadette was already getting feelings of the spiritual as we climbed the stairs to go to the top floor, where there was a large sitting area right outside the Robert MacKinnon room. George then showed us the third-floor ballroom and the adjacent room, where there had been many more experiences with the entity of Molly MacKinnon. I got a very odd feeling when I was in the ballroom; I felt like something was watching us. I don't consider myself psychic; however, I've been on enough investigations that I'm starting to recognize when we have something abnormal occurring. The last place we visited was the basement, where George mentioned another paranormal investigation group had one member come face-to-face with a dreadful floating ghostly face that caused the man to run from the Church House shrieking in terror.

It was getting late, so Bernadette called the group together and decided where to place the cameras. The Church House was so large that we'd have to break it into two separate investigations. The cameras would be placed in the blue room, the bottom of the first-floor stairwell, at the top of the stairwell on the second floor and in the Robert MacKinnon room. On top of that, the teams would be carrying hand-held cameras to get stuff as they roamed. Each camera would be night vision, and for the first time, the hard-wired static video cameras were going to be connected to the new large flat-screen monitor that would show all the cameras at the same time in color.

It was now 10:45 p.m., and George planned to stay in the kitchen while we made central command in the hallway just outside the blue room. We gathered together, clasped our hands, formed a circle and said our prayer of protection before the investigation began. The first team going in included Bernadette, Kate, David and Len. Mike, Ed and I would stay back in ghost central and watch the monitor, logging anything we thought might be paranormal.

Team one started in the blue room, and right away, the orb activity picked up. This continued as the group went out into the foyer, with a colorful pulsing orb that was floating right above Bernadette and following her and the rest of the group. There was tons of orb activity on the grand staircase, with them going up and down, and Mike remarked that one followed the path of the stairs all the way up to the second floor. While we were sitting, a bat swooped out of nowhere, making me duck to the floor. Luckily, Ed and Mike were able to chase it away with a broom.

An orb hovering by Paranormal Ed Livingston in the Church House's servants' quarters.

A spirit light orb hovering above the grand staircase at the Church House.

Team two would be Mike, Ed and I. We went immediately up to the second-floor landing, where Mike had brought the spirit box. I had the handheld digital recorder, while Mike was operating the handheld digital video camera, and Ed was using the K2 meter. I sat quietly while Ed peppered the spirits with an array of questions like "Are you a male or female spirit?" and "How many of you are there?" and "It would be nice if you would speak with us tonight." I didn't get any feelings until we went up into the third-floor ballroom. We would be off camera to the ghost central crew, but Mike had the hand-held camera, so we proceeded. The room was large and devoid of any furniture, and I could only imagine the glorious parties and dances the MacKinnons had held in there. I pictured Molly smiling and dancing in her flowing gown. I didn't get the same feeling as before, but that would soon come when we went down the hall from the ballroom, where there is an assortment of small rooms. These must have been the servants' quarters, for there was a small staircase that snaked its way down to the kitchen and basement. In this area, I got a feeling we were not alone, but I didn't experience anything paranormal.

We went all the way down to the basement and spent a quick fifteen minutes in there, but I didn't see a floating face, as others have. However, on the way, Mike's walkie-talkie started acting wacky. At this point, I took a digital picture of him, and above Mike to the left is an orb. We finished up, and everyone pitched in to carry the gear back out to Len's and David's vehicles.

Everyone marveled at the investigation and the huge amount of orb activity that had been going on. It would be interesting to see what revealed itself to us in the evidence we gathered. Many times, our best evidence is found after the investigation.

The Church House was so large that the Ghost Seekers of Central New York decided to go back for a second helping of paranormal experiences. This time, we had a crew of four composed of Bernadette, David, Paranormal Ed and myself. We wanted to focus on the third-floor ballroom and the servants' quarters, which were adjacent to the ballroom. Little did we know the evening we were going to have when we began our investigation on the night of September 15, 2012. It was a brisk and cool Saturday evening, and we arrived right after dark. We met George, the historian of the Church House, who brought along his loyal dog, Adam, a friendly pooch that was rather large and filled out his harness with his black-and-brown canine girth. We carried all the equipment up to the second floor and decided to make an office into our central command. Adam, the sweet and loyal dog, went up the stairs but then refused to go into the ballroom. I snapped a picture of him looking at something that we couldn't see. George commented that the dog was acting differently and behaved like he didn't want to be in the Church House, which is never the case. Bernadette commented that animals are great detectors of the paranormal and unexplained, much like children.

After running all the wires and hooking up all the cameras, we discovered that the hard drive that records everything refused to turn on. This device had worked flawlessly on the previous investigation. We would have to go old-school bare bones, with David working the hand-held digital video camera and Ed and I taking digital pictures. Ed would also carry the Gauss meter, with Bernadette and I each utilizing a hand-held digital recorder for electronic voice phenomenon. Going into the investigation, I had a strange feeling we might see the spirit of Molly MacKinnon or at least something unique. Little did I know how profoundly intuitive my feelings have become in regard to the otherworld.

We held hands and said our protection prayer, which always eases my mind. Bernadette led us up to the ballroom and talked about Molly's coming-out party, which had been held in the ballroom over one hundred years ago. When we were in the ballroom, we discovered someone had left a ladder that went into an opening in the ceiling. I climbed it with my digital camera and recorder. I looked in and realized I was in the attic. There were random socks nailed to the rafters, and I could not even fathom why someone would do that. It was bizarre, to say the least. We took our places in the dark, and I looked at my watch—it was just past 10:00 p.m. Bernadette started to ask the spirits questions, and it didn't take long until we all heard thumping coming from the hallway outside the ballroom and toward the servants' rooms. It was repeated a couple times, so we all got up and moved in that direction. I followed Ed and Bernadette, and we walked into a column of cold air at the hallway entrance into the servants' quarters. After taking a few steps farther, something caused Bernadette to stop in her tracks. She commented that something was holding her frozen to the spot. Finally, she was able to free herself from this paranormal shackle, but David was in the exact location a few minutes later and felt compelled to stand with his back against the wall. He stated that something wasn't right in that location. The Gauss meter was spiking in this area, which told us something was there. When we were standing in the hallway looking into the ballroom, I mentioned that I saw something move in the dark.

Right after my event, Bernadette walked out into the hallway and saw a figure move across the same area. She described it as not a shadow person but a figure made translucent that she could see through. There was no doubt we were dealing with something not friendly, for when we went back into that area, I ventured by myself into the adjacent room to the ballroom stage. I was within twenty feet of where Bernadette had seen the figure when something happened that shook me to my soul. I was alone in this room in complete darkness when something flowed through me. The only way I can describe it is as if a spirit walked right through my body. I knew something was wrong when my stomach started to churn, as if I had eaten a bad tuna salad sandwich. Then, as soon as the spirit walked through my body, every hair on both my arms stood up, and I had goose bumps all over my body like I've never experienced in my life. It was so bad that I walked out and over to Bernadette. I held my arms out and asked her to verify what had happened. She touched my arms and said that indeed my arms were lumps of bumps and the hairs were electrified. I don't know if I can truly describe how scary the experience was, and whatever caused it didn't feel friendly whatsoever. With Ed right behind her, Bernadette walked bravely into the room to face it down. She calmly talked to the spirit and said we were friendly. She explained that we meant no harm and we were there in respect and to help them. We packed up our gear and headed to the kitchen, where we said our closing prayer in which we ask no spirits to follow us or attach themselves to our beings. I was never so happy to pray. We headed out the door just after midnight.

The next morning, I attempted to listen to the digital recording I took, but to my shock, the equipment had recorded nothing but hours of hissing sounds. Once again, a failure of the equipment resulted in disappointment. It had to have been on purpose. This malignant spirit did whatever it could from its dimension to keep us from recording the verification of the existence of spirits in the house. I cannot explain it any other way. To say the Church House is haunted would be an understatement. Bernadette mentioned the presence of a vortex on the third floor near the servants' quarters, and I have to agree with her. Something just wasn't right up there. If you ever get the chance to tour the location, I ask you to tread lightly and be strong in mind and spirit, for the weak minded and easily led could be dragged to the darkest depths, a place our souls were not meant to be.

ADDITIONAL OBSERVATIONS FROM BERNADETTE PECK

The Church House proved to have spirits that lived up to the reputation and beauty of the grand structure. In the walk-through prior to the investigation, we were told about the ghost of Molly MacKinnon, and I was hoping we would get a chance to meet. The building was so large that we decided to split the mansion into two investigations. The first was on May 26, 2012, and as soon as we all walked in, I felt a spirit in the office. A creepy feeling came over my entire body, followed by the sighting of a shadow person. Although we didn't see Molly, perhaps the intelligent orb caught on night-vision video might be her earthly representation. Skeptics and other ghost hunters dismiss all orbs, but this spirit light orb moved with intelligence as it traveled slowly up the stairs, across the landing and then up the second set of stairs, the entire time pulsing and flashing. This spirit light reappeared over my head when I was in the dining room, or what we called the "blue room" because of the ornate blue wallpaper. Dennis had a pit in his stomach when he was in the closet of one of the servants' rooms on the third floor. He snapped a picture of "Paranormal" Ed at that moment, and an orb is right next to Ed. We were able to record some clear EVP, including "just a little" and "thank you," and when I asked if there was anyone there from the Borst family, I got a clear "yup." The most shocking EVP happened right after we got an answer of "eight" in response to a question about the number of spirits. Ed stated, "Don't be shy," and a clear-as-a-bell ghostly voice answered back, "F— you!" If anyone questions whether cursing is only an earthly voice violation, well, ghosts swear, too.

We returned to conduct the second investigation on September 15, 2012, and we had a smaller team composed of David, Ed, Dennis and myself. As soon as we walked in, we had equipment failures and malfunctions. Again, the bulk of the paranormal activity was up on the third floor, in the servants' rooms down the hall from the ballroom. We picked up EVPs when I asked if somebody was there. "Yeah," said the ghost. I asked the spirit if it wanted to tell us something. "No," came the clear answer. We heard movement and saw a shadow figure crossing our grid. The laser grid is composed of red lines that can show the movement of something dark across a pitch-black room. The Gauss meter was spiking, and David did something I rarely see: he freaked out. He was compelled to stand with his back to the wall as he sensed that something was not right up in the servants' quarters. It was moments after this that my body became frozen. I was standing and paralyzed to the spot. I could not move. I could not speak. I could not defend myself from the spirits of the night. As soon as I relaxed and was able to move, Ed picked up a ghostly scent that he described as paranormal cotton candy. My assessment was that the Church House is highly paranormal, with heavy energy—some dark and some light. I did not witness the ghost of Molly, but I know her spirit was there with us.

Chapter 5

ENCORE OF THE STANLEY THEATER

Utica, New York—Saturday, March 16, 2013

The clouds hung low over Utica as Mother Nature held on to her last grip of winter in the rugged Mohawk Valley. The Ghost Seekers of Central New York entered the hallowed stage of the glorious Stanley Theater for a return performance of the paranormal. The Stanley Theater is located on Genesee Street in downtown Utica. It opened in September 1928 and has a seating capacity of 2,945. The interior is in the Mexican Baroque style and is a marvel to view, with gold leaf–covered columns and a grand staircase that's fashioned after the one that had been on the *Titanic*. It's the crown jewel of Utica and right in the center of downtown. The Stanley is vibrant and active every week with stage plays and musical acts, and it hosts many proms and wedding parties. All are attracted to its grand elegance.

THE RETURN

This investigation was done with the most equipment that the Ghost Seekers had ever brought and set up. On the mezzanine would be a four-way monitor that would have four night-vision video cameras hard wired. Down in the lobby, we set up the large flat-screen monitor that had six night-vision cameras hard wired so we would have a total of ten cameras strewn in various locations of the Stanley Theater. We brought the entire crew of Seekers and two special

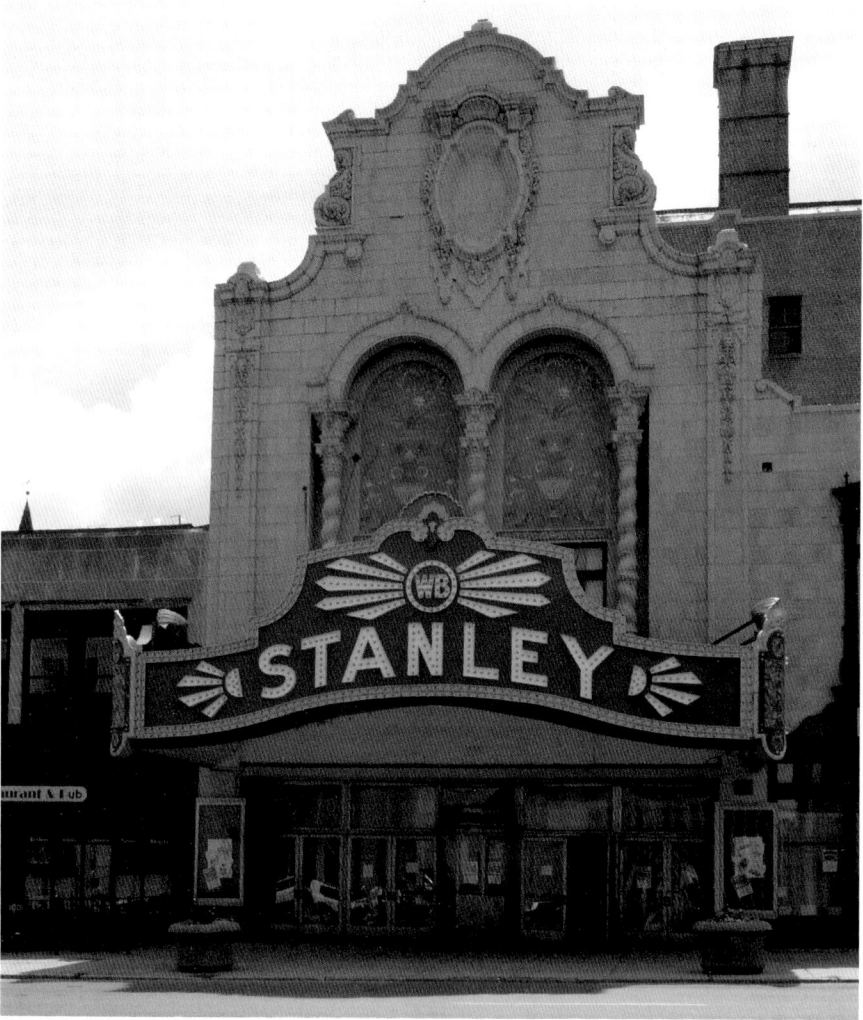

The Stanley Theater, the crown jewel of Utica.

guests, as the theater is haunted and vast. We had a lot to cover, and we had Bernadette, David, Paranormal Ed, Carol Pearo, Helen Clausen, Len, Josh and myself, along with the psychic Irene and a helper we will call Linda.* We had investigated the Stanley years before and had captured on video a ghost walking the basement ladies' room. We also had numerous paranormal experiences, so we were excited to get back in there and verify the previous findings, as well as make new otherworldly discoveries.

We performed a sweep of the entire building under the escort of the maintenance man, Bob Baker, a sweet and grizzled man whose ripped forearms are adorned with the faded tattoos of his youth. Bob told us that he was all alone on the mezzanine one evening in the dark, making his rounds, when he heard a voice over his shoulder say, "Excuse me." Bob stated that every hair on his body rose. He scrambled to the light switch, turned it on and found nobody there.

Bernadette had previously met with Monica, the manager of the Stanley Theater at the time. She had a ghostly encounter of her own. Monica told Bernadette that she was walking the mezzanine with a new employee when, down the hall, they spotted a man just standing there. The place was locked, and nobody was supposed to be inside. "Can I help you?" Monica asked the man, who turned, looked, walked away and disappeared into a wall. The ghostly interaction rattled the new employee so much that the young lady quit on the spot. Monica also mentioned that when she was alone in the tunnels underneath the Stanley, she heard voices and talking, yet nobody was there. One time she was in the downstairs ladies' room with another person discussing the upcoming investigation by the Ghost Seekers of Central New York when she heard ghostly breathing. Then—and this is common when you run into an entity—her entire body became ice cold. Monica stated it came over her quickly, and her legs felt like icicles.

When the Stanley went through a remodel some years ago, the tales of ghosts flowed from the construction workers. One was from workers installing new carpeting who had become spooked. When they were in the theater at night all alone, they would hear otherworldly music playing, although there were no musicians visible on the stage. One female carpet layer stated that she was hearing her name being called and started to have a conversation when she came around the corner and nobody was there. The ghosts scared the Mexican workers who were adhering the gold leaf on the lobby pillars—so much so that they ran screaming from the theater, yelling, "*Fantasmas Asustadizos!*" (scary ghosts).

The sweep got underway at 10:30 p.m., and the building was eerily quiet, except for the slight hum of the cooler in the mezzanine area. Bernadette, Dennis, Helen, Carol and Irene got the tour from Bob. People often ask, "Why do a sweep before an investigation?" The reason is to get a baseline. We need to bring along the K2 and the Gauss meter to establish where there might be electromagnetic interference of a natural source. These devices can spike from electrical appliances, junction boxes or outlets. We also had

Above: A massive orb spirit light ascending the grand staircase.

Below: Paranormal investigator Josh Aust is seen with a spirit light hovering overhead while conducting a ghost inquiry on the grand staircase.

Irene dictate psychic feelings as Bob showed us where everything was located and the hot spots of reported activity.

It was interesting to see the belly of the Stanley, to walk the bowels beneath the stage and beautiful displays. There are tunnels that run under the seats and under the front of the building and Genesee Street. I was able to look up a ladder, through a mesh metal vent and see the lights from the sidewalk. I was so busy gawking that I almost forgot we had a sweep to complete. Helen was carrying the Gauss meter and was detecting spikes in areas that were not natural. The theory is that if you get an unnatural spike in electromagnetism, it could mean a ghost is present. Even before the sweep, I detected spikes in the Gauss meter in the lower seating area in multiple rows. It was as if the ghost were an usher sweeping the rows. Irene picked up a lot of activity but especially concentrated on the downstairs men's room, suggesting that the smoking room, right outside where the urinals are located, had been host to something violent, perhaps a tragic death. She put the year of this event at 1936. Bernadette claims not to be psychic but certainly has a paranormal personality twinkle. I have been on many investigations with her, and in my own opinion, she is psychic. She always finds the hot spots and in this case felt uneasy in the tunnels, an area where we would hear ghostly footsteps later on.

We returned from the sweep, and Len, David, Josh and Paranormal Ed had finished running all the wiring for the cameras, hooked everything up and were putting the finishing touches on the technology that would attempt to capture the existence of the afterlife. First, we gathered together on the main staircase so we could have a group shot. Having our photo taken on the

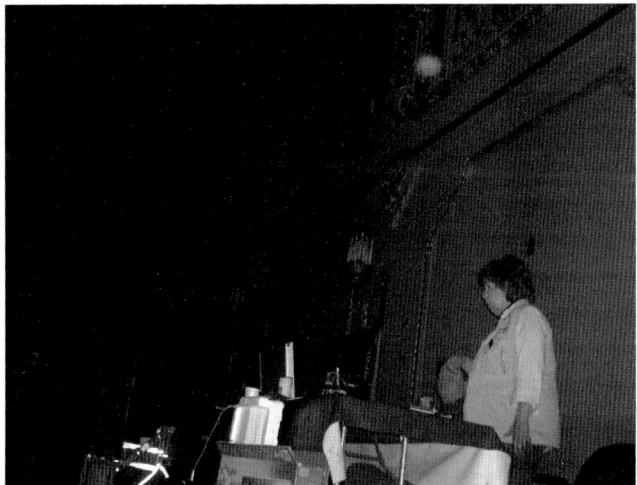

Paranormal investigators Joe Ostrander and Bernadette Peck run "ghost central" while a curious orb hovers above them.

Paranormal investigators David Peck and Carol Pearo follow voices and ghostly footsteps down the Stanley tunnel.

grand staircase was a cherished experience. We then stood in a large circle and held hands. We included Bob, the maintenance man. Bernadette led us in a prayer of protection so only the good spirits, the friendly ghosts, would come out and interact. We have no qualms about wanting to avoid dark energy or evil entities. We are not demonologists or exorcists; we are seekers, hence our name of Ghost Seekers. Once the protection prayer was completed, we broke up into three groups. Group #1 was composed of Bernadette, Helen, Josh and Irene. Group #2 included Len, Linda and Paranormal Ed. Group #3 was David, Carol and myself. The Stanley was so large that we each could take a different floor and would not interfere with one another. This way, we could cover a lot of the theater. Group #1 went upstairs to the balcony and the mezzanine. Group #2 covered the downstairs ladies room, and Group #3 went into the tunnels and the orchestra area of the stage. I was excited to get into the tunnels, as we were not able to conduct anything in that area during the last investigation. Bernadette and Irene both had the feeling of something down there, and Helen had been able to pick up something on the Gauss.

The tunnels were dark and musty and had the slight hum of an electrical panel. After only about ten minutes into the EVP session in the tunnel, David

The tunnels of the Stanley proved most haunted and had many paranormal occurrences, like the pictured orb drifting.

and Carol heard whistling. Because of the hum of the electrical panel, I could not pick up the whistle. Right after that, all three of us heard footsteps down the tunnel that leads from the downstairs bathrooms and under the seats to the stage. The footsteps were loud enough that David and Carol got up from their spots and wandered down the tunnel. It was impossible to detect on the digital recorder as the electrical hum drowned out everything, but all three of us heard the footsteps.

We then moved into the downstairs men's bathroom and smoking room. We were there for a good half hour and experienced a wide range of encounters. Right off the bat, Carol got a spike on the K2 that went from a baseline of 0 right up to a 6.3 and then right back down to 0. It was as if the ghost sprinted right past her. We discussed it and decided to go up and retrieve the spirit box. This is a device that searches radio frequencies that might be the host of ghost speech and broadcasts the words. This can sometimes result in an intelligent interaction and discussion with a ghost. David set the device up, and we all started to ask questions of the spirits. At this time, the temperature in the room dropped five degrees as I felt a chill right next to me. It was at this point that we picked up a scream on the spirit box.

We had been there close to an hour, so we decided to go back to ghost central and meet up with the rest of the team. When we got there, however, the other two groups had not returned. We decided to go up the stairwell by ghost central and conduct an EVP session until everyone got back. David took his flashlight, shut it off and placed it on a wooden sill by the stairs. During the EVP session, Carol asked for the spirits to turn on the light, and they complied. The theory is that the spirit energy will power the bulb, causing it to illuminate. David thanked the spirits and asked them to now shut it off, and they did. Once again, David asked the ghosts to turn on the flashlight, and they did. Spirit lights were photographed on this stairwell, which was the location of the most amazing paranormal incident of the investigation. When the other groups came back, Bernadette, Helen, Irene and Josh were showing everyone digital photos of a shadow person walking down the steps. They were able to capture two successive pictures of the dark walker.

There was no doubt the spirits were out to play on the stage of the Stanley. Unfortunately, Len, Linda and Ed were not able to really encounter anything in the downstairs ladies' room. This was surprising since the last time the Ghost Seekers were in the Stanley, most of the paranormal activity happened in this area. This means the haunting of the Stanley is an intelligent one; in other words, the ghosts are interactive and not residual. When we say a haunting is residual, it's like an entity imprint or recording, in which the spirit does the same thing over and over in the same place, like an otherworldly record player. It's not like ghosts are on demand. Len, Linda and Ed experienced something that happens to us all on various investigations: nothing. Of course, sometimes there can be ghost voices from the other side not heard until you listen back, so it was possible there could still be paranormal activity. Perhaps the spirits had been lady ghosts who were shy about men being in the ladies' room.

It was getting late, so the groups took a quick break, formed into new configurations and then went back out for another round of spiritual hunts. On this round, I teamed up with Josh and Helen. We decided to hit the stage. You would think that would be the place where there would be a lot of ghosts—up on stage, performing plays in the afterlife—but we got nothing. That was odd to us, as previously there had been activity on the stage, but suddenly they seemed to have moved on. Josh and Helen claimed it was a flat area. We didn't experience anything until we returned to the mezzanine and stairs. In the area by the grand staircase, where we had our group shot, we encountered all sorts of paranormal activity. Helen and Josh both said they felt a heaviness in their chests. We sat on the steps and were conducting an

An insidious black mass moves up the stairwell with a massive spirit light in the midst of the maelstrom.

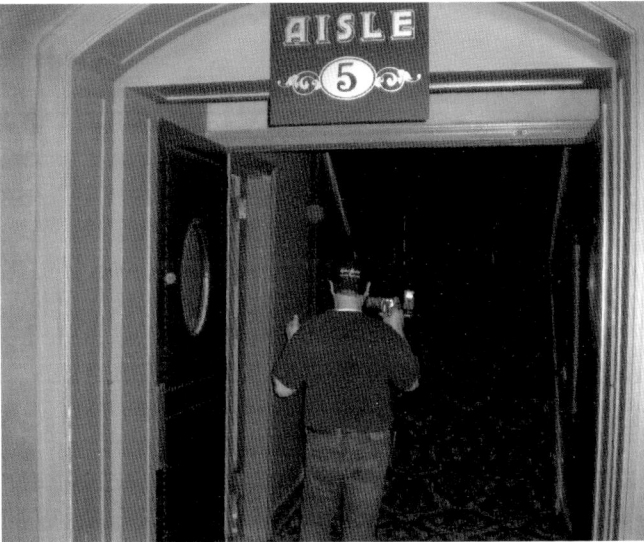

Josh Aust following an orb.

EVP session when Josh said he felt something behind him. Helen commented that she could see a spirit light right above Josh. I took a picture, and there it was, a pink-colored ball of spirit light a few feet above Josh's head. We then heard knocking, so we got up and moved down the mezzanine. Josh and Helen were asking questions, and both were getting responses back that told us it was an intelligent haunted response. We could not debunk it. At this time, we picked up an EVP. I was carrying a hand-held digital recorder, and on listening back, Helen made the statement, "I'm too old for this." A ghostly voice from the other side intelligently responded, "This is crazy." My theory on why the staircases are haunted is that they are the location of a massive amount of happiness. Wedding photos of families are taken there, and the audience ascends and descends them with joy and laughter.

Last Investigation

The final chapter for the investigation of the Stanley occurred on a cold, rainy and windy night on May 25, 2013, and the fun and lightness of the previous investigations turned dark and ominous. The evening's group include Bernadette, David, Len, Ed, Helen, Carol, myself, Josh and Joe, as well as special guest investigator Linda.* Irene the psychic would once again join us for a night none of us would ever forget.

We were greeted by Stanley Theater accountant Amy Lamberto, who told us some chilling tales of her own paranormal experiences. She stated that the coat rack in the office would move, and once while going down the side stairs to the street, she had been pushed from the back, as if a devious phantom had wanted her to fall.

We got the gear in place and embarked on the investigation, with the teams heading off in different directions in the large structure. I was with Bernadette and David on the first round, and we started out by going onto the stage. Being on stage in complete ink-black darkness was very unsettling, and right away David said he did not like the feeling up there. I took a picture at this moment, and it revealed a large spirit light hovering right above David's head. The Gauss meter spiked up to 2, and Bernadette heard voices. We decided to sit below in the blackness of the seats. We relaxed and started talking and asking questions of the possible spirits. It was at this point that we heard a growl coming from the rows to our right. It was so dark I could not even see my hand in front of my face, yet we all could feel the tension. It was obvious that the spirits were in a grumpy mood. Bernadette started her otherworldly communication with the ghosts by stating, "We come in peace," and immediately the temperature dropped from seventy-two degrees to sixty-eight degrees. You could feel a chill pass by then, and within seconds, the temperature went back to the original level. We decided to go back to ghost central, which was located in the front lobby, where Joe was all by himself. Joe told us that when he was sitting in the dark, watching the monitors that were displaying the night-vision video cameras, he had heard breathing and voices to his right, which is one of the grand staircases that has been a paranormal hot spot on all past investigations. It was at this point that Joe pointed out something spectacular on the night-vision camera that was pointing at the seats in front of the stage. We could see a ghost sitting in one of the seats. The camera was showing the back of the head of this entity that was waiting for a ghostly performance. The apparition was fading in and out. I had the feeling the growl was this spiritual patron, who was not pleased with us bothering him or speaking during the performance. At this point, Bernadette and I took a quick peek back into the darkened seat area, and she spotted a shadow person walking across the stage. We both heard loud breathing.

We marveled at this and paused for a few moments before we had to move on. We decided to go to the top of the grand staircase and run the spirit box. Sometimes the words captured on the spirit box are random, but many times we get a spiritual connection and intelligent answers. It was at this point that my sensitive nose picked up the scent of what I can only describe as French toast. We started the spirit box, and David asked if the spirit had a name. We got the answer "Mike." After a few minutes, I tipped my hat and said in a joking tone, "I'm going to keep wearing this hat, Mike. How do you like them apples?" Within a second, Mike answered back, "They're bad," which made us all chuckle.

We all got back together at ghost central to relay our experiences, and Len, David and Carol said that when they were in the upper balcony they got a very large K2 spike up to 7. That is incredibly high, meaning that a spirit was trying to manifest itself.

The scariest interaction happened in the basement ladies' room when Josh, Irene and Helen were assaulted mentally and physically by a dark entity that appeared in over a dozen digital photos as a black spiritual smudge that covered their faces and surrounded the investigators. This was exciting but kind of scary, as we are not demonologists. Helen was under duress and had to flee the basement tunnels to get away from this angry entity. Irene had felt during the previous investigation that there was terror and anger in the area, and this time it seemed to manifest and interact.

For the next round, I went with Len and Linda to the projection room. It proved to be flat and without incident, so we moved on to the upper balcony. It was up there that we had knocking in response to our tapping. Then something amazing happened: when Len was speaking, a ghost usher shushed him. This came out clear and loud on our digital recorder.

THE SÉANCE

During the last round of the night, the group decided to conduct a séance a few rows from the stage right in the middle of the seats. We gathered chairs in a circle in the aisle and placed a lit candle in the middle. Right away, we got interaction—Joe had his hair touched, and Len had a spirit touch his leg. We could all hear steps across the stage and a growl in the seats. This was the moment we would capture the growl on a digital recorder. We had heard it previously in the same area, but this time we captured the evidence. Bernadette felt a cold breeze, and Irene saw the vision of a ghostly janitor dust mopping the stage. Could this be Mike? I had the feeling the growling could've been Mike the janitor, grumpy at earthbound humans interfering with his spiritual duties. We surmised that he had been amused and playful at first but then had enough of us meddling mortals.

After discussing their experiences, it seems that Len, Ed and Linda had come across something paranormal in the ladies' room. Listening back to the digital recording of the EVP session in the ladies' room, a distinctive ghostly moan is heard on the recording.

The night came to an end, and I felt like my soul was exhausted as we had investigated every nook and cranny of this grand old hippodrome. I would say that the Stanley Theater is a very haunted place where the ghosts are more than happy to put on a show for us, the earthbound public.

ADDITIONAL OBSERVATIONS FROM BERNADETTE PECK

The multiple investigations of the Stanley Theater resulted in a massive amount of paranormal activity that would satisfy any ghost junkie. It was a pleasure and an honor to be allowed into the grand Stanley, and our paranormal appetites received ghostly desserts. Jerry Kraus, Stanley executive director, was kind enough to allow us back inside the wonderful theater. On our return, I, along with other investigators, witnessed a ghost man standing against the wall up on the second-floor mezzanine. He moved and then disappeared. The chandelier above our heads started to move right as we headed to the ladies' room, and it was as if the spirits followed us in there, as we heard male and female ghost voices whispering. Then, it happened: one of the stall doors slammed shut, startling the crew. We picked up some terrific EVPs, including "Hey, yeah" and "I don't know either."

The tunnels down below yielded some great evidence when David and Carol heard footsteps, whistling and screaming. This same whistling would be heard in the orchestra pit within minutes of the tunnel incident. Irene and Josh had a scary interaction with a dark energy that enveloped them down in the tunnels. It was following them down the tunnels, and we captured this in several photographs. You can see the progression of this black mass, and it was frightening to see it after the fact. The video camera David was using kept going in and out of focus, and Len's four-way monitor malfunctioned up on the mezzanine. This was the same night and area that Josh and Ed heard knocks along the walls. The stairwell we call the "*Titanic* stairway," used for many bridal party photos, had a large black mass moving up it, and we captured this phenomenon on our digital cameras. In the back second-floor business office, Josh and Irene heard a ghostly whimpering, and then Irene had a spirit reach out and touch her on her back. It was near the stairwell that leads to Genesee Street that we heard dragging and witnessed a black shadow person ascending the stairs. I was personally touched and felt the presence in that back stairwell, an incident that was rather dark.

Irene watched the six-way monitor, which had the feed of all the night-vision video cameras, and witnessed and chronicled some very interesting paranormal events. She watched numerous flashes that were not cameras. She described them as flashing and scurrying orbs, along with intelligent moves, that went up and down stairways and followed the investigators. A batch seemed curious about Ed and trailed him in the downstairs ladies' room. The ladies' room seemed to be a paranormal focus area. Len hunkered down in there and shut all the lights off. At the same time, the night-vision camera caught an orb that flashed and moved with purpose down the stairs and toward where Len was sitting. The evidence was massive and surely proved that the Stanley Theater is indeed not only haunted but also a paranormal cornucopia of otherworldly events piercing the veil of our mortal realm. It was a thrilling time to be a Ghost Seeker.

Chapter 6

PLAYERS OF UTICA THEATER

Utica, New York—June 15, 2013

Flames raged into the night sky. It was May 5, 1999, and the home of the Players of Utica on Oxford Road in New Hartford, New York, was gutted by a fire that destroyed everything from props to memorabilia. The charred remains of a loving theater would have to be demolished, and the largest unsolved fire in the history of Oneida County caused the players to scramble for a home. Little did they know that the final newly constructed building would host a play of the ancient kind: a performance of the ghost.

The Players of Utica started humbly in 1910 as a social gathering of Uticans wanting to perform for the amusement of their friends and family. It wasn't a community production theater company that entertained the masses until 1913. The Players of Utica is the oldest continuously operating community theater troupe in New York State and one of the oldest in existence in the United States. The tragedy of the fire led the group to fundraise in order to erect its own new home within the borders of Utica. The new building couldn't be constructed, however, until two structures were demolished on the selected spot on State Street. One was a private residence where rumors insist a person had been murdered, and the other was one of the oldest churches in Utica. The teetering wooden building with the crooked steeple had been host to St. Volodymyr the Great Ukrainian Catholic Church from 1948 until the group built its new church and moved out with the blessing of the new church on September 25, 1977. The Ukrainian group of Catholics

The Players of Utica building in the heart of Utica.

fled Eastern Europe in World War II to escape religious persecution and fascism by communist Russia and the Nazis of Germany. Their homeland now under communist rule, the Ukrainians took advantage of the Displaced Persons Act, which was passed by the United States Congress in 1948. This paved the way for the Ukrainians to immigrate to Utica. They had the assistance of their Ukrainian brethren who now resided in Utica. Most were so poor that they arrived in Utica with nothing but lint in their pockets and love in their hearts. The parish was incorporated in 1951. The church on State Street had previously been the home of St. George's Episcopal Church, which was built in 1862 and was the second-oldest church in Utica. It was constructed in the early Gothic Renaissance style. On Easter Sunday in 1952, the first divine liturgy was held by the Ukrainians. Eventually, this group scrimped and saved and built a new church in the Ukrainian style on Cottage Street in Utica. The State Street church fell into disrepair and, after decades of rot, was torn down to make way for the Players of Utica Theater.

The church had rumors of tunnels. During the demolition, the church was crumpled down into the cellar and covered over by dirt, and then the new Players of Utica Theater was built right over the top. This caused the spirits to stir, and the theater now hosts a massive amount of paranormal

St. Volodymyr the Great Ukrainian Catholic Church, which was torn down. The Players of Utica building now occupies the land. *Courtesy of Oneida County Historical Society.*

activity packed into a small playhouse erected for the enjoyment of the entire community.

Bernadette and I went to the Players of Utica Theater to meet with Vince Scalise, president of the players, on a cold, wet April evening in 2013. The building itself is a beautiful brick structure with the company logo proudly displayed on the front. Right next door is Tiny's, a popular club that has live music. The rest of the area is a closely packed group of family dwellings with friendly neighbors playing music and strolling the sidewalks. We sat at a table in the lobby with Vince while he told us a little history on the current structure. The ground had been broken in 2003, yet it took years for the shell to be erected and plays to be held there. Vince himself doesn't claim to be psychic, but from his personal paranormal experiences, one gets the feeling that his spiritual openness creates a personality gate that allows him to be a focal point. After years of doing investigations, you get the feeling that ghosts are much like children and animals: they tend to be attracted to the gentle ones, the ones who are open to new experiences. Vince went on to describe spiritual interactions experienced by volunteers, as well as his own. One of the volunteers is very sensitive to ghosts and told Vince that there is a spirit present that likes the theater and likes to follow Vince around. This would be proven later on in our investigation. Vince described how a lady came in wanting to borrow some clothing props, and she had her young son with her who kept pointing his finger up at the ceiling, laughing and seeming like he was chatting with something not seen by the naked adult eye. Suddenly, the mother turned to Vince with a shocked look on her face. When he asked her what was wrong, she said the spirit of a man had appeared. She stated she seemed to attract ghosts and this spirit man had revealed himself and gotten close to her face. She grabbed her young son's hand and fled the building without the props and was never seen again.

The freakiest story Vince told had to do with a little hide-and-seek game the spirits had decided to play with him. Vince always says hello and goodbye to the ghosts as he's entering and leaving the building. He goes to the facility a lot by himself. He was there one night and had unlocked the building and was finishing up when he could not find his keys. Nobody else had come or gone, and he had used them to let himself in. He could not find them. He searched and finally said to the spirits, "Just give me back my keys." Luckily, he had locked the doors on his way in so all he had to do was click the door shut and hope to find them in the building when he returned. Well, when he got home, the missing keys were on his desk.

Vince says the mischievous spirits have been known to stroke hair, pat the shoulders and touch members, patrons and volunteers. Many times, people hear wood clapping together in areas where there are no mortals of this realm. Chairs are moved and costumes thrown from their hangars. Vince felt the ghosts were not dark entities but curious, playful and happy to have artists in their midst.

The investigation took place on June 15, 2013, on a warm summer evening. When we arrived, the mood was jovial and optimistic. We placed ghost central outside, as the theater was small inside and we didn't want investigators making background noise. The ghost central location was ideal, as people could chat, drink coffee, smoke cigarettes and wait to hear what happened as each group went inside. We stood in a circle in the lobby, held hands and conducted our opening prayer. The first team of David, Joe, Helen, Irene and Players of Utica president Vince would go in. While waiting to go inside, I enjoyed watching the night-vision cameras. While the first team was in the building, I was shocked at the massive amount of spirit light activity going on, especially in the room where the stage was erected. This is the temporary stage since the main stage is still in an incomplete phase of construction. But this is where the players had been having their shows, and now the spirits were showing off for the Ghost Seekers. The rest of the group out at ghost central marveled at the display. We know the difference between dust, water droplets or bugs and actual paranormal floaters. The spirit lights were drifting up and down, back and forth, with all manners of throbbing, flashing and spiraling. I had never seen anything like this, not in terms of pure numbers and nonstop activity. This went on for the entire forty minutes that the first team was inside.

When the team members came out after their session, they were ecstatic at the amount of activity they had experienced. Vince had been the focus of the spirits, but the team also picked up some interesting responses on the spirit box. Joe had asked if the spirit smoked. A clear "yes" was picked up. Then Joe followed up by asking what brand of cigarettes the ghost smoked. The answer blurted out of the spirit box was "Pall Mall."

I was excited to get into the theater and experience the dance of the performancing phantasm. Team two would be myself, Bernadette, Josh and Carol. Team one had concentrated its efforts in the area of the theater where all the props and costumes were hanging, so we decided to go to the right of the theater, where the temporary stage is erected and all the current plays are being performed. Carol sat in a chair on the stage while Josh walked around with the hand-held video camera. Bernadette was speaking

Players of Utica president Vince Scalise, seen here without any paranormal activity captured on film.

Players of Utica president Vince Scalise was photographed mere seconds later, enveloped by spirit lights from another spiritual plane.

to the spirits while I was snapping a few digital pictures, and I was thrilled when I captured a massive, multicolored spirit light hovering right over Carol's head. Right after this photo, Carol reported that she felt something on her neck and her hair raised. Bernadette saw something moving across the back of the stage, and the Gauss meter spiked up to 4. Bernadette approached the spirit and tried to speak with it. She stated, "This was holy ground, and now we have performance of the ghost." We sat down to do an EVP session, and within seconds, I saw a shadow movement down the hallway by the dressing rooms, and then Josh spotted movement in the corner. Bernadette sensed a lot of ghosts in the room, with a lot of paranormal activity, and was getting the name Josie. We decided to place a flashlight out on the table on the stage, and several times when we asked questions, the light illuminated in response.

There was no doubt that we knew the Players of Utica Theater was haunted. We moved off the stage and down the hall to the back of the theater, where the performers would dress and rehearse before going on stage. In there was a couch that Bernadette and I sat on while Carol and Josh sat across from us. The floor was bare concrete, and within seconds of settling in, the ghosts would use it to provide a once-in-a-paranormal lifetime thrill. It was so dark that I could not even see my hand in front of my face. Bernadette had just taken a digital photo in which an empty chair had a large spirit light sitting in it when we heard something being thrown across the floor. It came from the left of us where there was no one present. I quickly shone the flashlight toward the sound, and it was a pencil that was still rolling across the floor. The noise of the wood pencil bouncing on the concrete was picked up quite clearly on our digital recorder. Within a minute of this, Bernadette talked to the spirits and said, "Don't be frightened." In response, I heard what sounded like a breath or huff that was about a foot behind and above Bernadette's head. It startled me, and when we played back the moment on the digital recorder, it was clear and distinct. There was nothing behind her but a solid wall; the other investigators had been across from us.

We took a break and then went back in with the group consisting of Bernadette, Helen, Josh and myself. We went into the area of the costumes and props, where we captured many spirit lights, including a cluster around me when I sat in a little prop chair. The best interaction with this group happened when we went back to the temporary stage area. Within a minute of sitting there, we heard spirits walking behind a large wooden panel over by the wall. At this time, Vince came in, and we asked him to stay with us. The spirits seemed to enjoy his company, and the activity jumped in his presence. I took a couple digital photos of Vince sitting on the edge of the stage. One picture was totally clear, and the next, taken within seconds of the other, showed a massive amount of spirit lights and orbs all around him. It was as if he were the earthbound conduit and mortal comfort to the ghosts of the theater.

While sitting on the stage, Bernadette felt something lightly brush her arm. The feeling, she said, was as if a spider web were being dragged across her forearm. Bernadette and Helen kept stating they felt that something was on stage with us, and Bernadette said she saw something moving on the back corner of the stage. Within seconds of this statement, David and Joe came in to try to debunk what they had seen on the night-vision camera out at ghost central. They had picked up what looked like a shadow figure standing in the corner and moving right to where Bernadette had pinpointed it.

At this point, everyone took a break to stand out in front of the Players of Utica Theater and sip coffee and take a few drags on their cigarettes. Everyone in the group marveled at the sheer amount of paranormal activity inside the quant little theater. We all agreed that the love Vince had for the building and the performances of his players brought forth much activity.

The last event of the evening was a séance conducted on the temporary stage where the bulk of the spiritual activity had been occurring. Irene had

Carol Pearo sitting on stage with a large spirit light looming.

Séance on the stage at the Players of Utica Theater.

brought a large candle with an image of St. Michael on it, and the little flame was the only brightness piercing the ink-black night inside the theater. Josh and David skipped the séance so they could start picking up and packing up the equipment. It was well past the witching hour, and the ghosts were ready to perform for us. We all held hands, and Bernadette and Irene led us in a chant. It was during this moment that I could feel a burning energy surge through my hands. It was freaky, and I really struggle to describe it. It's like nothing I had ever felt outside this circle. We unlatched our hands, and within a minute, Bernadette started to get a sharp pain in her side, and then something touched her leg. Irene felt a spirit behind her, and when I snapped a quick digital picture, a large presence could be seen looming over her shoulder. Helen then had a sharp pain in her right leg, ankle, side and arm. Helen started to hold her digital camera up and snap pictures over her shoulder. She captured what can be described as a shadow person wearing a hat with a brim. We finished up, held hands and conducted a closing prayer in which we thanked the spirits and asked them to not attach to us or follow us home.

There is no doubt in my mind, as a paranormal investigator, that the Players of Utica Theater is haunted. So, dear reader, beware, for the next time you sit in the audience at the players' performance, you might just have a ghostly friend sitting in that empty seat next to you.

ADDITIONAL OBSERVATIONS FROM BERNADETTE PECK

In our walk-through, we were told by Vince of the activity that had been happening at the theater. A woman had seen the spirit of a black man in the back area of the unfinished part of the theater. The witness to the ghost fled from the theater and has never returned. Vince and some of his board members had reporting feeling odd and uneasy in certain parts of the theater. Vince had also felt the energies of the spirits in the theater by being touched and stroked by ghosts. I knew the Players Theater would be a fantastic investigation as I had that paranormal twinkle that comes to me on occasion, and this happened on the sweep and included the Gauss meter spiking. My instincts and Vince's experiences were enough to warrant the ghost hunt.

The night of the investigation proved to be active from beginning to end. Right off the bat, Irene heard whispers, and Helen saw a shadow person hovering above David, along with a hovering sable mist. We all heard footsteps, and Joe felt a cold breeze blow across his body. There were no fans or building ventilation of any kind. Joe's interaction with the ghost responding to the type of cigarettes indicated we had an interactive intelligent haunt. It was at this point that Vince became overwhelmed and had to leave the building. It is rare when ghosts make physical contact with our world, as in the pencil-throwing event. The séance proved to be the paranormal capstone with the group hearing voices, knocking, walking behind a nearby panel and Helen having a shadow figure in a black hat hovering behind her. Irene's digital recorder provided some amazing EVPs, including the names Pat, Kevin and Nick. The best part of the session came when we asked who the spirits were and received the ghostly answer "priest" and "preacher." When we asked if the spirit was a preacher, the same voice answered, "Why?" Then Irene asked if the spirit needed help, and "I do" was the response. David asked if the spirit wanted us to leave, and a female responded, "Get out." Then Joe asked if the ghosts had seen Vince, and the response "Yup, I did" was returned. The questioning continued, and the ghosts said, "Vince." The best part of this EVP session was that the Players Theater had been built on the grounds of a demolished church, and we had a ghost saying it was a priest.

Being in the Players of Utica Theater was a pleasure and privilege. I hope we get a chance to come back and play theater with the spirits.

Chapter 7

A RETURN TO MUNN'S CASTLE

Utica, New York—July 9, 2011

On a mild summer evening, the Ghost Seekers of Central New York returned to Munn's Castle on Rutger Street. The Ghost Seekers investigate many places, and a select few are so overflowing with paranormal activity that they get another investigation. Munn's Castle certainly fits into the category of highly haunted locations. Munn's Castle was named after the original owners, John and Mary Jane Munn, who purchased the property and built their castle in 1852. It was designed by Alexander Jackson Davis, one of America's most revered and important architects of the nineteenth century. The plans to Munn's Castle are well known among designers and are preserved at the Metropolitan Museum of Art in New York City. It is in the Italian Villa style, with a brick exterior wall coated in a sand-and-paint mixture. It has marks scored into it that give the appearance that the home was built of large stones. A well-known resident was Samuel Remington, the famous American gun maker. The home was converted into a nursing home in 1952 by Mr. and Mrs. James Dowling, who named it the Dowling Nursing Home. When modern-day visitors are going through the castle, they note that many of the eldercare accoutrements are still in place, including tubs, bathroom cabinets filled with bedpans and some rooms with patient beds stripped down to the bare mattresses.

The only difference with the return of the Ghost Seekers was that this time, I was along for the investigation to record our findings firsthand. I was nervous, as I had heard from Bernadette that the place at 1 Rutger Street was highly haunted and had provided the group with a thrilling and spine-

Munn's Castle at 1 Rutger Street in Utica.

chilling paranormal investigation. As I pulled up to the mansion, I noticed that its gravel driveway, long overgrown with grass, still had distinctive tire ruts leading up to the stone steps and the large arched front entrance. I parked next to Leonard Bragg's vehicle and found him already inside with some of his equipment. My cellphone rang at that moment. It was David Peck calling me to say they were right around the corner. I felt a chill although it was a summer night with no wind of any sort. I had brought along my digital camera and was compelled to take a photo of the castle. As soon as I snapped it, I found my eyes looking up to a second-story window that gave me the willies. I swore I saw something moving in the window, yet Len was now coming out the front door. There was nobody else in the castle, but when I later reviewed the picture I took, I could see a faint ghostly face looking down on me. It was as if my paranormal instincts had come to life. With each investigation, I feel I'm starting to tune into the spirits, although I don't consider myself anywhere near as tuned in as Bernadette.

When the entire team arrived, everyone was in great spirits. The team going into the bowels of Munn's Castle included Bernadette; her husband, David; Paranormal Ed; Leonard Bragg; Kathy Durr; Kate Geary; and Mike Geary. Everyone was assisting in carrying the tripods, cameras, cords, a table and a four-way monitor, as well as large tackle boxes on wheels that hosted a multitude of devices, batteries, duct tape, flashlights and many other ghost hunting tools. It was 8:45 p.m. when the team entered the house, and I was blown away by the gracefulness yet visible age of the magnificent structure. The front archway entrance was many feet taller than me, and the entrance room had gorgeous architecture to it that made me marvel. I could only imagine the souls that walked the castle since it was rather old. To the left of the archway was where Len placed his folding table, which would hold the four-way monitor. Mike, Ed and David were assisting with the snaking of cords to the hotspots within the mansion.

I thumbed my crucifix as I stepped to the parlor on the right. Of all the investigations I had been on, this would be the first time I ever had worn it. It gave me comfort, as Father Kelly had blessed it back in 1992. I set down my small duffle bag, which held a couple bottles of water and all of my ghost-hunting accoutrements.

It was at this point that Bernadette called us together to do the pre-investigative sweep of Munn's Castle. Mike, Len and David kept stringing extension cords and did not accompany us on the sweep, leaving Bernadette, Kate, Kathy, Paranormal Ed and myself to walk the massive castle. We walked by the beautiful spiral staircase that reminded me of a staircase down to Hades. It spiraled upward into the dark and ominous heart of the castle, though I couldn't see any farther than the beginning of the second floor. We walked past a suit of armor at the base of the spiral staircase, standing at attention as a guard to the other world. We walked through the adjacent rooms on the first floor, and when we got to the back room that was right off the kitchen, Ed's K2 started to spike and go from faint yellow, past green and all the way up to red, letting us all know that there was spiritual activity, for it was not near any electrical appliances, cords or any other device that can set it off. We climbed the spiral staircase to the second floor, and right away I felt uneasy—right at the moment that Bernadette was speaking of the place having been a nursing home. Bernadette is the archivist and researcher for the group, as she always has the backstory of every place we investigate right in her mind, including names of previous occupants and tragedies that had happened in the location. Munn's castle certainly hosted death and despair on numerous occasions.

We went up to the third floor and into the scrying room. Scrying is when a person will try to channel the spirits through a medium like water or a mirror. This was the room with the mirror in which Bernadette and Kate had seen spirits on the last investigation. There's no doubt in my mind that this is the creepiest room in the castle, as it has a small adjoining room that you had to duck through the entranceway to get into. The adjoining room was a small, unfinished room with rafters above your head and small built-in shelves that had religious statues right below a small window. We called this the "religious room."

The next place we went was up the narrow and creaky wooden steps to the crow's nest, which was really hot and dusty. It was in this peak of Munn's Castle that Ed's K2 pegged all the way to the red indicator light. Bernadette was satisfied that the walk-through was thorough and complete, so we all headed back downstairs, where the guys had finished setting up their gear, shut the large front doors and placed a two- by eight-foot board across them, barricading us inside. It was time to conduct the protection prayer. Bernadette had brought holy water, and we all took turns blessing ourselves before we held hands, closed our eyes and listened to our leader pray to the spirits to bring us no harm and to follow us to this realm. This was 10:00 p.m., and we were now ready to break up into teams and begin the paranormal hunt.

The mansion is rather large, but Bernadette and the crew members knew exactly where to place their equipment based on their past paranormal experiences. Video camera one was placed in the second-floor bathroom, video camera two was placed in the back room on the first floor looking into the kitchen, video camera three was placed up by the crow's nest and video camera four was placed in the first-floor living room. Team one was composed of Ed, David, Kathy and myself. We went right upstairs to the second floor, and Ed brought along a trigger object; that is, an object placed on a floor or on something to try to get the spirits to interact and move the item. Ed had brought along a water bottle that was half full, and he placed it balancing on its cap so if a ghost barely brushed against it, the bottle would fall. I brought upstairs a little toy car. Bernadette had brought along a wine glass and placed it in one of the first-floor rooms that had a fireplace, where she put it on the mantle, dusting talcum powder lightly around the edges so if a spirit moved the glass even a millimeter, it would be noticeable. Ed and I placed the trigger objects in the middle of the floor, and everyone hunkered down to begin the EVP session. Sometimes a ghost will respond to questions in a voice that the mortal ear can pick up, but other times, it will speak in a frequency we cannot detect until later when the recordings are placed into a computer program. While the EVP was going on, David had his hand-held night-vision video camera recording the entire session.

After ten minutes, we moved into the third-floor scrying room and repeated the same EVP protocols, except this time we were able to shut the door to give us complete blackness. In no time, Kathy stated she did not feel well in the room. A few feet away from where she was sitting was a door that opened up to what we called the "religious room." Kathy said she didn't fell well as she was tuning into something that made her uneasy. As soon as she walked out of the room, I snapped a picture that later revealed a large orb hovering in the doorway to the religious room.

We went back downstairs and reported our experiences to Bernadette and the group. Team two was now formed of Bernadette, Len, Mike, Kate and I. Being the chronicler of the ghost-seeking experiences, I get the privilege of going on both teams in case something really juicy happens. Bernadette had us bring along all the trigger items, as well as the powder and our K2 and Gauss meters. Bernadette led us right into the first-floor foyer. She used her paranormal nose like a bloodhound on a scent trail. She's tuned to the other side, and the rest of us follow her lead. We went into the kitchen in the back of the first floor and received some K2 hits, as well as some blips on the Gauss meter. As we left, Bernadette sprinkled powder to see if we'd get ghost tracks. We were leaving the kitchen going to another first-floor room when we received on the audio ghost app a spirit that gave its name as Dick. Mike challenged our new friend by saying, "C'mon, Dick!" Right after this, Mike saw a shadow person moving in a back room, and Bernadette confirmed this, although I was bringing up the rear and missed it. "Why are you here?" asked Bernadette as she led the group, the hand-held digital recorder picking up any EVPs. We then went into the first-floor room with a fireplace that we were told by the Landmark Society of Utica was used for entertaining guests. Bernadette and Kate decided to hold hands and dance, twirling themselves around and giggling. We all smiled, and I figured this would lure any ghost from his hiding place, for the joyful memories of the dance are one of the things that spirits miss from our realm. It was within a minute that we got another name: Martin. When we moved toward yet another room, we picked up the name Rose and then the number sixty. Bernadette and Kate picked up a dark entity moving toward the basement.

It was in the basement that I was to get the most chilling paranormal experience of my life. The time was close to midnight, and we had just returned with team two when Ed, Kathy and David asked me to venture into the basement with them. I had downloaded the ghost radar app onto my cellphone. As a group, we do not put much credence into these apps and would not use it again on any investigation, but what was about to happen was either an odd coincidence or paranormal intervention. I brought my phone with the ghost app as we ventured down the creaky old wooden stairs that gave me the creeps on the first step into the bowels of the building. The basements in these mansions are always creepy, and Munn's Castle is no exception, especially since it was built before the Victorian age. As soon as my feet hit the basement floor, the ghost radar started blurting out words and showing a massive amount of colored blips on the screen. The words spit out within a minute were the following: ghost, black, both, arrange, pain and army. The ghost radar became silent as we sat, and Kathy started the EVP by asking the spirits if they were in pain to turn on the flashlight. Kathy had turned off the flashlight so only a ghost entity could power it on. When she requested the ghost to turn on the flashlight, it came on. We all decided to walk to another part of the basement, which proved difficult because the pitch black was darker than octopus ink. I was right behind David, and Len and Kathy were behind me. It was at this point that I walked into what I can only describe as an extreme cold spot. The basement felt balmy and was sealed, with no windows to allow breezes. This cold spot wasn't moving. It was as if I had stepped into a walk-in freezer. All the hairs on my arms raised, and I had goose bumps all over my body. I was carrying my ghost radar in my hand, along with my pad of paper and my writing implement. As soon as I walked into the cold, the ghost radar said, "pencil." I mentioned how cold I was, and Paranormal Ed snapped a picture. Later, when we were upstairs, he showed me that you could see a distinct streak of white going between my arm and body, ending on the pad of paper I was holding in my hand. Right after this, Kathy's flashlight came on, and then it all ended abruptly.

When we got back upstairs, Len received a complete name on his ghost radar. "Jeff Dutch" was what came out, and when Len asked if his nickname was Dutch, the ghost radar answered right away with "never." It was past midnight, and Bernadette led the last group upstairs that was composed of our leader, myself, Mike, Kate and Ed. We hit the second-floor rooms that had been missed. Munn's Castle had been converted to a nursing home for a short period decades earlier, and these rooms had cheap hospital beds that still had the soiled mattresses on them. I got the feeling of sadness and death in these rooms. It was in one of these rooms that Bernadette and Kate picked up the presence of a man not of this earthly realm, and then Kate heard a ghostly whisper in her ear that said, "Cold." Len picked up "excellent" on the ghost radar and then "doubt" as we moved to the stairs.

Lastly, we returned to the scrying room where, when we were doing the EVP, Mike and I again heard footsteps out in the hall, yet there was nobody up on the third floor but us. We went into the religious room off the scrying room, and when I went into the religious room, Bernadette and Kate were channeling the spirits. I took a digital picture that had two different-sized orbs. One was large and geometrically shaped, while the other was smaller, brighter and round. When we all got downstairs, there was a buzz out front among David, Ed and Kathy. They were out on the lawn of Munn's Castle and had witnessed a UFO buzz right over the mansion. These are steady, honest, hardworking folk that in my experience do not make things up or exaggerate. If they claimed to see such a thing, I believe them wholeheartedly, and so should you. So we had an unidentified flying object (UFO) right over Rutger Street in Utica at the same time ghosts were active.

When we all walked back into the mansion to take down the equipment and pack it in for the night, Bernadette called us over for one more surprise. The wine glass with the powder around the base had been moved about a quarter of an inch. Nobody had been in the room all night long, so it had been touched by the hand of a thirsty ghost perhaps seeking one last mortal sip of wine.

We held hands, performed our closing prayer and walked back out onto the front lawn. I looked one last time at the windows of Munn's Castle, where the spirits of the departed view our world from another plane of existence. I felt sad that a great investigation had come to an end.

Additional Observations from Bernadette Peck

We had been in Munn's Castle on multiple occasions, and the spirits never disappoint. It's as if they wait in the empty mansion for us live folk to arrive to communicate with or attempt to frighten. My team of investigators and I have been on many ghost hunts and are not so easily scared. The night of July 9 was no different. When we were in the library, we asked if there was a mistress present and got an EVP that said, "Cora." Then we asked if this were a female energy answering and received a very clear "yes." We tried to pass the spirit along, but she was too fond of the mansion and said, "No." Later on, we were in the scrying room upstairs, and I felt a stalk of cold air that was a stark contrast to the summer heat. It was at this time that we got the chilling voice from the other side saying in a growl, "Get out!" When we left the room, we had another strong EVP saying, "Goodbye." We had a sighting of a very large shadow person walking in the small room that is off the kitchen, and we continually heard footsteps in the expansive halls. There were knocks and whispers in multiple locations. Dennis, Ed, Dave and Kathy had a paranormal interaction in the basement, where they could feel a moving mass of frigid air that followed them around, and at this time, Ed took an amazing picture of Dennis that had ectoplasm swirling around his body. They all heard a loud spirit voice that said, "OK." The wildest event was at the conclusion of the investigation when we were outside and David and Kathy spotted a UFO hovering over Utica and especially above Munn's Castle.

OTHER HISTORIC HAUNTS OF THE MOHAWK VALLEY

The rest of these investigations did not take place within the borders of Utica but rather close by within the gouged-out landscape that is the Mohawk Valley.

Chapter 8

THE NEWPORT MASONIC TEMPLE

Newport, New York—August 17, 2013

The shadow person stood in the back corner of the main chamber, peeking, peering and wandering among our solid bodily existence. This would be among the many ghostly interactions the Ghost Seekers of Central New York would have on a lovely summer night in the town of Newport.

The town was first settled in 1786 and is nestled in Herkimer County along the banks of the glorious babbling waters of the West Canada Creek. Newport is lined with Victorian-era mansions and the Amish traveling down the road with their horses and buggies. I came to know the Masonic Temple when I was asked by the Kuyahoora Historical Society to give a presentation on my book *Wicked Mohawk Valley*. Eric Newman was there as the Masonic Temple hosted the discussion. Afterward, I asked Eric if there had been any paranormal events in the building. It was a marvel both inside and out, and I had a good feeling there could be something. He said there was no reported activity, although rumor had it that a Masonic brother had passed away many years earlier up on the second floor.

I myself am a Mason, so I knew how precious and sacred this temple was to fellow brothers. Eric was kind enough to let the Ghost Seekers come and ply our trade in the building to see if there were spirits hanging around. I did explain to Eric that in death, many times, spirits will go back to places of sadness or happiness. Although the building had been constructed for the exclusive use of Masons, it had hosted over a century of friendship, fellowship and happy times by the leading men of the community. Although women are not allowed to be Masons, the temple has a ground-floor dining hall, game room and kitchen that host all the family events for men, women and children in Newport.

The Ghost Seekers came back to do a walk-through to see if the place warranted an investigation in mid-May. Bernadette, David, Irene, Carol and myself were there as Eric gave us a personal tour through the temple. Upstairs, in a sitting room right outside the main ceremonial room, Irene had a strong, heavy feeling in her chest, and right by the swords that hang on the wall, our K2 meter went up to a 4.9 where just moments earlier there had been nothing. The Masonic temple was built in 1903 and is a two-story Colonial Revival mansion that has five bays and is listed on the National Register of Historic Places.

It was the middle of August on a mild summer evening when the Ghost Seekers of Central New York descended on the Newport Masonic Temple to conduct our investigation. Driving through the picturesque town of Poland and into Newport, one smiles at the scene of small-town America that's rarely in existence in this age of skepticism.

We would soon have our paranormal skills put to the test. Our team was fully loaded with Bernadette, Irene, Carol, Helen, Josh, David, Len, Ed and myself. The sun was on the rim of the earth, and long shadows cast across the waters of the West Canada Creek, across Route 28 and on the temple as we lugged all our gear into the building to set up in the preselected areas chosen from the previous walk-through. We set up night-vision video cameras in the first-floor dining hall, the piano/pool table room and the foot of the staircase and then up on the second floor in the waiting room outside the main temple, where the swords were on the wall, inside the chamber and up in the attic. Setting up the equipment, running all the wiring and getting the gear on-line and recording takes hours, with David in the lead directing the charge.

Once we were ready, Bernadette assigned the teams for the first go-around. The place was so large that two paranormal investigative teams could be deployed at the same time and not spoil the other's investigation. Team one was composed of David, me, Helen and Irene, and team two consisted of Len, Ed, Joe and Carol. Each team had to have one investigator whose job it is to carry the hand-held digital video camera. Each team would have a K2 to measure spikes in electromagnetism, a digital camera and temperature gauges to measure sudden drops in temperature. Bernadette would stay back in ghost central and watch the four video cameras. This main station was located in the kitchen. Because of the sheer size of the

The Newport Masonic Temple.

Ghost Seekers Dennis Webster and Paranormal Ed Livingston reflected in a mirror at the Newport Masonic Temple.

temple, we had to place a substation up on the second floor. The length up to the attic was too great, so that camera and the ones in the temple would be wired into monitors in the hallway by the top of the stairs. I was with team number one, and we went upstairs to start by the sitting room where everyone was getting spikes on the K2 by the swords hanging on the wall, including a high spike by Len as we were setting up. The spirits were ready to engage. Within a few minutes of sitting down, Irene felt pressure on her throat and a strong feeling that women are not welcome. This was followed by Helen getting a chill.

After a while, we decided to enter into the main ceremonial chamber that is sacred to Masons. When in ceremonial session, no women are allowed. We were only a few steps inside the chamber when Helen had an angry entity slap the flashlight out of her hand. She was struck with such force that the flashlight went flying at least ten feet in the air and landed next to my feet. Her hands started to tremble and tingle. It was jarring and shocking. Then as we settled down, Helen's camera would not allow her to take pictures of certain objects inside the temple chamber. The camera continued to work just fine as she pointed it at other investigators, the walls and the chairs, but each time, nothing was caught when trying to capture holy objects. It was as if a Masonic brother from the other side was forbidding her from documentation. I decided to knock three times in the hopes of a ghostly return knock when David's camera lost focus. Upon listening to the digital recordings, you can hear a distinct knock in response. Irene and Helen sat to the side, and Irene felt a spirit hand touching the top of her head. I saw a dark mass the size of a basketball fly right over my head. Helen asked the spirits to send us a sign. As soon as she concluded this sentence, I had something slap me on the top of my head. Within minutes, there was a *whump* on the wall right behind Helen and Irene. David mentioned that he had the feeling of many spirits in the room. He couldn't see them, but he could feel them.

Joe and I are Masons, so we decided to go into the ceremonial room all by ourselves. I brought in an old-fashioned black bowler hat and set it on the altar. Joe and I asked many questions of our passed-away brothers, and nothing seemed to be happening until, upon the conclusion of the query, I went to pick up my hat. It had a dent in the top, as if a ghost fist had slammed down on it.

For the conclusion of the investigation, the entire team went up into the attic. The rafters were well above our heads, and there was a strange wooden room built into the corner that none of us could guess what it had been used for. We went and sat in there for a few minutes, asking questions, but Bernadette felt pulled into the larger room, so we decided to move out there. Within a few minutes of settling down, we got an EVP of "What is it?" in a very low ghost whisper. The flashlight beam was coming on in response to questions. There was no doubt there was paranormal activity in the area. Bernadette sensed children hanging back in the corner and got up and approached them, asking, "What is your name?" She also said, "Don't be scared. We are not here to harm you."

It was at this point that we picked up on the digital recorder a ghost whisper that stated, "They're afraid." Irene felt the spirits of the children were playing hide-and-seek, a spiritual game that made me wonder if fun and play is common in the afterlife. Joe and Ed started saying, "Marco!" and then "Polo!" when we heard a shuffling in the corner. David, Helen and Bernadette heard footsteps over in the same direction. We all heard something stepping right behind Irene.

We finally concluded the investigation, turned on all the lights and began to reel in all the gear when Joe discovered his beloved Masonic pen was missing, making the group wonder if a ghost Masonic brother had borrowed it to scribe notes in the afterlife—or perhaps to play a prank on an earthbound brother.

Ghost Seeker founder Bernadette Peck walks toward ghostly children's voices while multiple spirit lights and orbs hang in the rafters.

ADDITIONAL OBSERVATIONS FROM BERNADETTE PECK

It was honor for me and the entire group to be allowed to conduct an investigation inside the hallowed halls of a Masonic temple, and the Newport one would prove to be a thrilling and fun investigation. We had spirit interaction that Len recorded with his video camera of the flashlight coming on and off intelligently to questions asked. We had a lot of large spikes on the K2, including a strong 4.9 in the wardrobe room right outside the main second-floor hall. It was in the hallway next to the main second-floor temple room where everyone heard footsteps of the ghost while there were no living souls in there. We had thumps, Irene heard voices, Dennis had an entity smack him on his head and Helen had something slap the flashlight out of her hand. In the first-floor billiard room, we picked up a moan right at the time Irene said she felt ill. We picked up some clear and fantastic EVPs that included one spirit asking, "Can you shut the lights off?" We asked if the ghost was mad and received a clear, "Yes."

The best interaction was toward the end of the investigation when we were up in the attic. I had the feeling that children were up there, and we could all hear childish whispering. When I stated for the children not to be afraid, we picked up a clear voice from the other side saying, "They're afraid."

Chapter 9

THE MADISON HOUSE

Oneida, New York—April 16, 2011

The day before our investigation, there had been sunbeams warming up the valley, but overnight the wicked wind came blowing in at a rate that broke branches. The clouds moved ominously overhead as rain poured into the darkness of the night. It was a spring evening, and I was heading out to Oneida to go on another ghost hunt with the Ghost Seekers of Central New York. This was a relatively close jaunt from my home, with less than a half hour drive, yet it seemed more dangerous with the stiff wind jostling my little car as I went up and down the hills of Route 5.

The town of Oneida is one of the most picturesque slices of America you will find, with Colonial-style homes lining the Main Street and a quaint downtown, of which the Madison House was part. It was among this scenery that I would be again seeking an interaction with spirits from another plane of existence. Even though the wind was harsh and the rain heavy and steady, my attitude was one of great anticipation for I had a premonition that this would be an investigation I would not soon forget. I was soon to have my instincts validated.

I parked my car in the rain and took a moment to take in the Madison House, marveling at the down-home look of the three-story historical structure that now housed a restaurant, pub and a few apartments. I had brought with me only a small pad of paper, a black medium-ink Bic pen and my Gauss meter. I had purchased this device recently and really liked it, for it has an audio beep and flashing red light that increases in frequency as the field gains strength. I would soon find out how important this device would be to the evening's investigation.

I walked into the Madison House and gave Bernadette a hug and David a hearty handshake. I was among my ghost-seeking friends, and I was grateful for the invite. Mike and Kate Geary were there, along with Len Bragg, Kathy Durr and Ed Livingston, or Paranormal Ed, as he prefers. We had to sit together and wait for the remainder of the diners to vacate the restaurant. We would be totally alone in the house, and the night couldn't be better for it. We sat and chatted about a wide range of topics, as friends tend to do.

As soon as the last person exited and we were given the green light, we leapt into action as we all carried gear into the building. I was amazed at how quickly the group could set up all the video cameras, tripods and cabling. I took a moment to stroll around the building, getting a base line with my Gauss meter. I had nothing set off my device, except the plugged-in coffee maker. Other than that, there was nothing. It was just after 9:00 p.m. when Bernadette handed me a printout on the history of the Madison House, and I read about the religious services held for Abraham Lincoln and Martin

The historic Madison House of Oneida.

Van Buren staying there, as well as tales of debauchery and prostitution. The building had hosted everything from elegance to malignance. I was sure this would mix into a paranormal cornucopia. The four-way monitor was set up adjacent to the bar near a couple couches and rocking chairs that were inviting and comfortable. Lincoln had stayed in the house in room #5, which for some reason was now #3.

We met in the dining room, and Bernadette gathered the entire team around and relayed the history of the Madison House and all the tales of people who had stayed in the historic building. I felt excited to begin the paranormal safari. We all stood up and spoke the prayer of protection, asking the spirits to come forward and stating that we meant no harm, that we were there on a mission of respect. We asked for protection from the dark entities that foul their dimension as well as ours.

I started out by going into the back first-floor dining room with Kate and Len. Before we sat down, my Gauss meter moved slightly, and Len declared that he was losing power to his hand-held digital movie camera. Kate set her digital recorder on a table, and we conducted the EVP session. After fifteen minutes, we got up and moved over by the entrance, and my Gauss meter went to a higher level, so we continued the EVP until it was time to get back to the command center. It was when we got back that I heard of a rare paranormal incident: Bernadette had witnessed a shadow person walking behind the bar. This entity would return later and be witnessed by Kate from another angle, and neither experience could be debunked. It was at this point that Kevin, an employee of the Madison House, came into the investigation and said that there have been sightings around the bar. This validated Bernadette's and Kate's experiences. This was a great start to the evening.

Bernadette and David went with Kevin to the kitchen area while I stayed with the rest of the group to monitor the four-way set up at the command center. This device shows four infrared night-vision cameras on one large monitor. We watched as orbs sailed through the darkness and then logged these occurrences for later review of the evidence. Sometimes, perceived orbs can be debunked as dust particles or insects and moths flying in front of the camera. I have watched these monitors enough to now recognize a true paranormal orb versus a false item.

The group bantered quietly on a wide range of topics, with a "look at that one" interruption every so often. When Bernadette and her crew returned, she was discussing with us that she experienced a dark energy by the door to the basement.

At 11:00 p.m., I went with Len and Paranormal Ed up to the second floor. It looked to me like they were your basic older apartments until we came to the end of the hall and went into an area under construction. We had to snake our bodies through freshly nailed studs and came to a back hall and rooms that looked to be untouched by remodeling for well over a century. There was no power, and the hallway and rooms were squid-ink black to the eyes. Faint dust and mustiness penetrated my nostrils. I walked the entire narrow hallway and got nothing on my Gauss meter. On the second pass is when the excitement began. All of a sudden, my Gauss meter pegged right to 5, which is the top of the scale for electromagnetism. The device was chirping like crazy. Ed had his night-vision digital video camera, and Len had the digital recorder, so they started right in with the questions to the spirit realm. Len asked if we would move down the hall, so we did, and the Gauss meter went dead. Then we stopped at the end of the hall, and after a few seconds, the meter lit up and chirped. Len asked me to go up with the device, and it shut off once it got to the height of a full-grown person. I then went slowly to the floor, and the device stayed lit and pegged all the way to the floor. I went left and right, and it would shut off once I went farther than the width of a human being. It was the perfect shape of a full-bodied entity.

"Fantastic," said Len. "Amazing," said Ed. They both started conversing with our visitor in their typical mellow and professional style. Bernadette and the entire team always maintain the proper ghost-seeking decorum regardless of the situation.

I said aloud that I wasn't psychic, but I had begun to feel queasy in my stomach. Bernadette had told me before that this is common when psychics are channeling and connecting with spirits. We then walked into one of the dilapidated, abandoned rooms. The Gauss meter once again was dead and lit up as if the ghost followed us into the room and stood directly between myself and Ed.

We returned to the base, and Bernadette, Mike and Kate decided to go up to the second floor to see what interactions they could get. I sat again with the others and watched the monitors, and we all had a fun moment when a little mouse was caught scurrying across the floor, his little beady eyes lit up in the night-vision camera beam. It was now 12:30 a.m., and I went along with Bernadette, Len, David and Kevin to the basement. The staff of the Madison House had found bones buried in the basement, so we were anxious to get down there and see what was rustling about. The steps going down were wooden and worn to the point of dangerousness. The basement was of the old stone type you see in very old Colonial structures and had a lot of rooms for storage of all kinds of decorative accoutrements. It was extremely dusty and creepy as we explored every nook and cranny. My Gauss meter never went off, but the digital recorder was going as we crawled all over the place. Len had put on a mechanic's jumpsuit and was attempting to get into a narrow crawlspace but was unsuccessful. We went back upstairs as it was getting late, but Ed asked me to go back with him up to the second floor to see if we could replicate what had happened earlier. We went back up there, and the gauss wasn't lighting up in the hallway, which meant the first visit was a true ghost interaction.

We decided to go into the room with the number 29 on the door. We hadn't gone into it earlier. When we walked in, my senses told me there was something in the closet at the back of the room. There were toys and children's clothes stacked and piled all over, so we had to slalom in the dark to get to the closet. As soon as I got next to the closet, my Gauss meter pegged to the top, lit up and beeped as loud as it would go. I couldn't see anything, but my feelings told me there was something there. I replicated what I had done earlier, and the meter lit up only when I outlined the form of a child of about four feet tall. I was frozen in place and didn't know what to do until the meter stopped as if the child had moved away.

On our way out the door, Ed noticed an exterior door that did not belong there and asked me to place the Gauss meter next to it. Amazingly, it lit up as if there were paranormal energy attached to the door. I could only imagine that the people who came and went from the Madison House through this door must have left their energy on it.

I would conclude the Madison House as a haunted location that had the best evidence in the shadow person that walked the bar for Bernadette and Kate to see, as well as in the spirit interaction on the second floor.

Additional Observations from Bernadette Peck

Being I'm from the area, I had always known about the haunted Madison House, and it felt great to be close to home on an investigation. The place would not disappoint. We were inside the restaurant setting up after the last patrons had left when David witnessed a shadow figure cross the entryway hall and walk and disappear right into the wall. I had spoken to the manager of the Madison House, and he had told me that motion detectors going off behind the bar all night was a common occurrence. It was in this exact location that I and others would get paranormal evidential payoff when a shadow person was witnessed by myself, Kate and others. It was as if the ghost were waiting for us to mosey up to the bar, order a cold beverage and chat about the events of the mortal world.

The hottest ghost interaction I had in the entire investigation was when I was in the back of the banquet room in the dark night. It was too dark to see very far, yet I sensed something moving about, something negative, and the K2 meter was hitting high marks, which means possible paranormal activity in the vicinity. In regard to the dark presence, I have conducted hundreds of investigation of the other realm and have recognized over the years when something is among us that just doesn't belong. This was one of those benchmark moments. I was with Kate when we both heard a distinct dragging across the floor.

The EVP session that I conducted with Kate and Mike was the creepiest and best evidence collected of the investigation. We used small hand-held digital recorders. We were also using the spirit box, and I was chilled to the bone at what we picked up from the Madison House. Kate and I asked, "Who is with us tonight?" and the voice from another world stated via the ghost box, "Deb." Kate asked, "Deb who?" and the last name "Forsythe" came to us. I was amazed by this, for Deb Forsythe was a person we all knew who had passed away years ago. We then got the name Phyllis on the spirit box, and I was moved, for this was the name of my mother. My brother James had passed away, and the spirit box also spoke out "James." It was my friends and family reaching out from a friendly, familiar location. The voice box also said, "Bernie," which is what my close friends call me instead of Bernadette. I felt that not only were we making contact from the other side, but they were also reaching out and attempting to communicate with us. It was a very emotional moment for me to hear the spirits of friends and family connecting their souls to mine from their ghostly plane. Mike and Kate had conducted an EVP session in the banquet room and picked up sounds of silverware rattling although the place was empty except for us Ghost Seekers and interactive spirits.

Another strange occurrence happened when the spirit box was left alone in the banquet room. Later on when we listened to it, we got some names and a chilling statement. Again, the names Nigel and Linda were spoken, as well as "Leave," but the most bone-chilling was a distinct different voice that kept saying, "Stop, stop, we are here," and another desperate third voice that stated in agony, "I'm in hell."

Up on the second floor, Dennis, Len, Mike and I experienced many cold chills and massive K2 electromagnetic spikes. Room #29 proved to be a paranormal hot spot, with us getting chills and high Gauss meter spikes. Also, the mini DVD video camera captured the sound of an upstairs door being opened. You can hear the distinct squeaking of a door opening followed by haunting footsteps of the dead, yet there was nobody up there. We had been told that the basement was a scary place, for some kind of bones had been found there. We discovered that the basement was in two distinct sections, and the bones had been found underneath the banquet area where the paranormal activity was hot. We had gone into the other section of the basement. In a follow-up investigation, I plan on delving into the belly of the dark basement and facing whatever spirits are hiding down there.

One thing that happens on many of our investigations is equipment failure. It is theorized that ghosts draw energy from electronic devices in an attempt to materialize in our dimension. The Madison House had many cases of flashlights blinking and going dead, even after fresh batteries had been placed in them, as well as Kathy's digital camera constantly turning off and Len's digital video camera shutting off on its own. On top of all this, many digital and video cameras were having autofocus issues. I sometimes wonder if the spirits are playing games with us and our equipment. Perhaps they're in a spiritual realm where they can reach out in order to gain back the earthly pleasures that are missing in their spiritual dimension. My assessment, as a paranormal investigator, is that the Madison House is absolutely haunted.

Chapter 10

HENRY HITEMAN ENGINE & HOSE COMPANY FIREHOUSE

West Winfield, New York—August 6, 2011

The mist was rolling in as I drove through the hills outside West Winfield. It was approaching twilight, and the humidity and rain of the early day had produced ominous fog that lay between the tree-filled mounds of earth as I wound down to the small town on the edge of Herkimer County. I was headed to the picturesque town of West Winfield, a town of just under one thousand residents that was named after General Winfield Scott. It's a quaint and beautiful small town comprising 0.9 square mile, with a branch of the Unadilla River running through it. Bernadette had called and asked me if I could accompany her and the Ghost Seekers of Central New York in investigating the firehouse on West Main Street. Back in the days before the New York State Thruway, traffic and people going east and west across central New York would transverse Route 20, which goes through the heart of the town. The travelers would walk right past where the volunteer fire department was erected.

Most of the communities in central New York have volunteer fire departments. These brave men and women rush to the aid of their families, friends and communities without any regard for their own personal safety. It's within one of these communities and firefighting buildings of brave citizens that ghosts patrol. The Henry Hiteman Engine & Hose Company of West Winfield was named after an early supporter and was founded on April 10, 1906. The mission is as stated: "To inculcate love of country, good citizenship, civic virtue and self-sacrifice, and to perpetuate the spirit which

The Henry Hiteman Engine & Hose Company Firehouse.

from the earliest days has actuated volunteer firefighters in the rendition of service of the highest type in the protection of life and property from fire, without the hope of fee or reward." It was within the walls of this firehouse that we would be investigating paranormal events.

I arrived at the station and strolled across the street, taking digital pictures of the building, as a few locals drove by, looking at the stranger with the camera with raised eyebrows. I went into the building, where Bernadette and the entire team were already setting up the equipment. Along with Bernadette was her husband, David; Kate and her husband, Mike; Kathy; Len; and Paranormal Ed. A new person would be joining the team: psychic Judi Cusworth. While Mike, David, Len and Ed were setting up equipment and running wires all over the firehouse, I followed along with Bernadette, Kate and Kathy as we did a walk-through, but first, we talked about the previous ghost sightings and otherworldly interactions with the fire chief and president of the department. We went out to the dining room so Judi could be sequestered, as she did not want to know anything about the building or the interactions. She wanted to go into the evening with a clean psychic mind. I stood back, scribbling in my notepad as quickly as I could, as Bernadette talked with Fire Chief Kevin Brown, President Jim Murphy and Jim's daughter Erin Murphy about their paranormal experiences. The chief and president were upstanding men who look you in the eye and shake your hand with a strong grip. These are the type of men who built this country and not the type to make things up. I felt everything they were saying was the truth. There's no other way with people like Kevin Brown and Jim Murphy. Chief Brown said that a few firefighters knew about the ghostly activity at the station, but not many more people in the community were aware. He also didn't let anyone know that the Ghost Seekers of Central New York were going to be conducting an investigation. He was afraid that pranksters would come around and bang on the walls of the building, thus spoiling the possible evidence that was to be collected. Chief Brown mentioned that firefighters working in the kitchen had heard chairs slide across the floor in the adjacent dining hall. He mentioned that in the eighteenth century, a hotel had been on the property. It had burned to the ground and then was replaced by two single-family homes. These were eventually replaced by the original fire station in 1910, which was added on to in 1970 and then finally razed and replaced with the new structure in 1992. Erin had been in the dining hall once and heard whistles right behind her, yet there was nobody there. Another firefighter had reported to the chief that he walked through cold spots in the kitchen. This volunteer firefighter described it as a column of frigid air. The kitchen has no windows or vents that could produce frigid air in that location. Others have reported doors opening and closing when they were all alone in the firehouse. Chief Brown described how he was all alone in the firehouse in the dead of winter when he heard the front door to the garage open and close. He didn't think too much of it, for the volunteers were always coming and going. He heard footsteps in the garage, so he decided to go and see who showed up on such a cold and blustery day. When he walked out into the garage, there was no snow from boots, so he opened the door to the outside, and there were no tracks in the snow.

We went out into the garage, and the chief and president pointed out an area in the back corner that had been a small jail cell in the old firehouse. It had been used in the days before the New York State Thruway when vagrants and hobos would walk through West Winfield. If these travelers had too much to drink and needed a place to stay, the fire station would serve as their hotel, with the most drunk placed into the jail cell overnight before being let go in the morning to head on their way. One morning, one of these vagrants was found dead in the cell, having passed peacefully in his drunken slumber. Chief Brown described an incident in which he and President Murphy were standing near this location when a black shadow mass in the shape of a ball flew right at them, making the chief duck. Near the back of the garage, President Murphy described seeing a shadow person with no legs moving in between the trucks. He walked the area, and there was nobody there. The chief mentioned that until May 1975, women were not allowed to be in the fire department and could only be members of the ladies auxiliary. Now, however, Erin Murphy is a member, and when she is alone in the truck area of the garage, she'll hear clothing moving. The chief feels that perhaps the ghosts don't understand why a woman is in the garage area that had always been for men only.

Back in the old days, the firefighters would come to the old fire station and play nickel point pitch, even retired members. The station was a focal point for these brave men, and their spirits were still fondly attached to the place. They were still coming around, keeping an eye on the living firefighters.

Another item of great paranormal interaction is the 1939 pumper that is parked in the middle of the station. President Murphy mentioned how this old pumper had once hosted one of the vagrants, who was found dead slumped behind the wheel. Another possibility of ghosts in the fire station is Norman Churchill, the founder and first chief of the department from 1906 to 1915, as well as Henry Hiteman, whose ghost was seen by a lady from the town. She had been walking by the station and had seen a man in early twentieth-century garb standing in the door looking at her. She didn't pay it much mind until she came into the station and saw an old framed photo of Henry Hiteman in the hallway. She pointed to it and exclaimed that she'd seen the long-dead man in the doorway. He even had the same bow tie and outfit on as what he was wearing in the picture. The strong emotional tie to the building was spoken about by President Jim Murphy, who stated with a lump in his throat, "This is a fun place but a stressful place. Life's highs and lows take place right here in this building."

We shook hands with Chief Brown, President Murphy and firefighter Erin Murphy as they left the building. It was getting close to 9:00 p.m., so Bernadette led the group on a sweep of the entire building. It was during this sweep that I had something creepy happen to me. I was a little bit behind the team, as I was held up writing something on my little legal pad. Like most writers, I tend to get lost in my world of words. I was by the boiler room that was in the location of the jail cell when I heard footsteps on the concrete floor. I stopped writing, took out my little flashlight and shined it in there, but the room was empty. Right after this, Kathy got a spike on her Gauss meter in the same location. It was a great sign of paranormal serendipity that we would encounter all night long.

The four-way monitor system was placed in the office of the chief with a few folding chairs in front of it. Bernadette led us in our opening prayer as we all held hands in a circle in the kitchen. I always feel comfortable and at peace after we have this prayer for we never want anything malicious or insidious latching onto our carbon mortal stalks.

We broke up into two teams, with one group watching the monitors, while I went with the other team, composed of Bernadette, Mike, Len and Judi. It was 9:15 p.m., and Judi had done a walk-through on her own with nobody telling her anything about the fire station. We headed out into the garage that had all the trucks, the 1939 pumper and the area of the old jail cell. Judi walked right to the 1939 pumper, placed her hands on the truck and closed her eyes. It was hard to see in the dark, but the illuminative glow from our small flashlights was enough for me to see what she was doing: channeling the spirits associated with this old pumper. She immediately gave the name David as being associated with the old truck. She then said there was a death associated with this vehicle, but it was not as a result of a fire or a firefighter. She was also picking up the name Penelope, which is not a modern name for a girl. Mike, Len and I were being quiet as Bernadette and Judi were speaking to the spirits when, suddenly, both ladies saw a shadow person standing down in between two trucks. It was at this point we all heard footsteps coming from the other side of one of the trucks. We followed Bernadette and Judi as they were slowly walking toward the shadow person.

"Hello," said Bernadette. "We mean you no harm."

Judi spoke slowly, "Who are you? Why are you here?" As we got closer, the shadow person moved away, around the corner of another truck. We all froze as Bernadette and Judi commented on this shy ghost that was keeping away from us. After ducking us for a while, the shadow figure disappeared as quickly as it had shown itself.

The next group to go out into the garage area included myself, David, Ed, Kathy, Kate and Judi. Once again, Judi, Kate and Kathy were witness to a dark figure darting between the trucks. When Judi asked its name, the ghost asked her, "Why do you need to know my name? You know who I am." Judi then said that there was more than one spirit in the garage and that they were just there to do their job. The spirits couldn't understand why we mortals were making such a fuss. They wanted to do their work. This gave credence to Bernadette's theory that old firefighters were hanging around what had been their favorite place in life. Perhaps they were hanging around the station to lend a hand or spiritualistic support to their living firefighter brothers and sisters.

Psychic Judi Cusworth places her hands on an antique fire engine as she channels the dead.

Later on, David and I went into the dining room to conduct an EVP session. The chief had placed on a table some objects that had belonged to the original fire chief: a uniform, a belt and a deck of playing cards. All these items were to be trigger objects. We set the digital recorder down next to the items. It didn't take long for David and I to bring out a string of words, including horse, sound, discussion, sing and arrangement, among others. When David asked, "What's your name?" the device answered "Mr.," causing us to chuckle since the spirit wanted formality.

It was past 11:00 p.m. when I went with Bernadette, Len, Kate and Judi into the dining hall to conduct an EVP session. Mike brought along the spirit box, and as the ladies were asking questions, we heard a distinctive, "Go!" After ten minutes, Judi and Bernadette had a strong feeling toward the hall where the men's and ladies' rooms are. They sensed heightened paranormal items in the vicinity of the ladies' room, with the lights coming on after Bernadette and Judi left the room. We also experienced cold spots in the hall, and Mike had the spirit box going.

After this, I decided to hang in the chief's office and watch the four-way monitor. It was interesting to see orbs floating across the screens from the night-vision cameras. Camera one, which was by the 1939 pumper, had a lot more activity than the other cameras, and from watching many times on other investigations, I could tell these were not dust or insects flying in front of the camera.

At this point, it was past midnight, and the group had investigated every nook and dark cranny of the West Winfield firehouse with a lot of documented ghostly interactions. This was Judi's first ghost investigation, and I was amazed at her accuracy. She seemed to click phenomenally with Bernadette and the rest of the group. She looked spent yet satisfied. She gratefully thanked the entire group for asking her to be part of the investigation. I could hardly wait for Bernadette and the rest of the Ghost Seekers of Central New York to go over the evidence and reveal what else came out of the other spiritual dimension.

ADDITIONAL OBSERVATIONS FROM JUDI CUSWORTH, PSYCHIC AND MEDIUM

As a psychic, the paranormal connection to the West Winfield fire station was very strong and clear to me. The first message I received was as I was on my way to the firehouse. I knew instantly that someone had suffered a fatal heart attack there because my own heart felt physically as if a ball of lead were inside my chest. Because of that, it was no surprise to me when I found more activity and clear messages once I entered the station. Upon walking into the West Winfield fire station, I immediately picked up several different energies throughout the structure and in several locations. At one point, I made contact with a male energy that appeared to be sitting in the corner of the boiler room. He had made it clear to me that this was not his first time being there. It was only later that I was told that this specific area had at one time been a holding cell, and many years ago, a hobo had spent the night in the cell and passed away in his sleep. After my psychic investigation, I would conclude that I was completely satisfied, with no doubt, that paranormal activity exists at the West Winfield Fire Station.

Additional Observations from Bernadette Peck

In my interview with the fire department volunteers, I learned that the Henry Hiteman Engine & Hose Company Firehouse had been the place of some rather interesting paranormal activity, including full-bodied apparitions, and the 1939 antique fire engine parked inside had been a conduit for the spirits. A humanoid figure that was described as dark, smoky and see-through had been seen by many of the firefighters. The night of the investigation proved fruitful, as evidence poured in all night from beginning to end of the ghost hunt. I was in the dining hall with Judi when we clearly heard a spirit say, "Go!" Len and Judi were walking around asking questions in their EVP session when Len asked if anybody was in the hall and got the response, "Hi." The night-vision digital cameras picked up twelve minutes of heavy orb activity. When we were walking out in the garage area of the trucks, I saw a shadow figure hiding and peeking around the front fender at our group. Judi and I approached and told the spirit we were friendly and meant no harm, yet the figure kept moving away from us as if it were the one that was afraid. David witnessed, and videotaped, massive orbs right after one of the investigators rang a fire bell. The aftermath of the investigation was interesting, as a male full-bodied apparition was seen by multiple people standing in the front door looking out into the street. There was another report of a volunteer seeing the ghost of a man who sported a scraggly goatee peering through the window. There is no doubt that this fire station has a paranormal twinkle and guardians of the firefighters staying about watching over their living brethren.

Chapter 11

THE SHACK

Sangerfield, New York—January 21, 2012

On a subzero winter evening, the Ghost Seekers of Central New York gathered at the home of Barry Lawson* to conduct what would become an evening of paranormal emotionalism not yet seen in the history of the group. Prior to the investigation, Barry had met with Bernadette Peck and investigator Kate Geary. He had approached the group with stories of fright in the home where he lived alone with his dog, Bailey, and his cat. He'd been seeing spirits on many occasions in his home since he moved in four years ago, and even his ex-girlfriend had seen them.

The home, at one time, was a nineteenth-century brick-making operation that locals had referred to as "the Shack." It had been converted to a home that now hosts the living and the dead. Barry had told the ladies in vivid detail about a little girl ghost, around nine years old, that he'd seen on several occasions, always accompanied by a short, stout, elderly spirit that seemed to either be protecting her or keeping her away from others, providing her no spiritual freedom to roam in the otherworldly dimension. He described the little girl ghost as having long black hair pulled into a ponytail, a blue period dress from a century ago and shoes with brass buckles. At one time, the little girl ghost touched him on the arm. The interactions that Barry was having occurred in all parts of his home. When he was alone in his kitchen, he had heard a spirit whistling in the backroom he has off the kitchen, as well as giggling. He has smelled strong perfume come and go when he is in the bathroom, which is a common paranormal experience with hauntings.

When his girlfriend was over to the house, she saw a shadow figure walking on the enclosed front porch that was locked from the outside. When Barry checked, there was nobody there.

During Christmastime, Barry was decorating his tree when the bottom half started to shimmy and shake, but the top half of the tree stayed silently still as if the spirit of the little girl ghost was assisting in the decorating. Barry had experienced waves of intense heat as if it the old-time brick-making kiln was firing up from another dimension and warming through to ours. One time when Barry was alone with his dog Bailey in his bedroom, he saw an elderly male spirit that had a potbelly, gray hair and suspenders. This elderly spirit was bending over, looking at the dog. This meant that Barry was having intelligent hauntings. Barry was extremely concerned about the little girl ghost being trapped, as well as the other paranormal happenings, so he reached out for help from a couple women who claimed to be paranormal investigators.

You must be truly careful whom you invite into your haunted house. There are many ethical and terrific ghost hunters out there, but there are also those who seek to exploit or perform investigations for the thrill or to entice and incite the spirits, even going beyond the bounds of good taste and expecting demonic interactions. People like Barry have no clue how to tell the great ones, like the Ghost Seekers of Central New York, from the exploitative charlatans. These immoral and improper investigators can go into a haunted location and leave paranormal damage in their wake, even if they mean well. Barry had these two young Goth ladies come into his home. They were covered in tattoos, wearing black leather clothing, snapping gum and twirling their hair. This would be fine as long as they took the investigation seriously, which they did not. They did pick up one great piece of evidence in an EVP that had said, "Hi, how are you?" The problem was that these girls left the home and stirred up the spirits. Nothing changed or improved for Barry, and certainly the little girl ghost was not helped in any way, shape or form.

It was through positive word of mouth that Barry had heard of the Ghost Seekers of Central New York and its many decades of ethically conducted spiritual investigations. He met with Bernadette and Kate, and the entire group knew this was going to be a sensitive and difficult investigation. How true this would turn out to be!

The night of the investigation was the coldest of the winter as temperatures plunged below zero. The team on site for the investigation included Bernadette, David, Kate, Mike, Josh, Paranormal Ed, the psychic Marlene

Marello and myself. For the first time since I have been investigating, the owner was going to be home and actively participating, as Barry decided to be there to work with us. As Mike, David, Ed and Josh set up the gear, Bernadette led Kate, Marlene, Barry and I on a sweep of the entire house. Marlene came in cold, as she knew nothing about Barry's experiences. For those who are skeptical of psychics, I say seeing is believing, and Marlene Marello is the real deal. She walked through the house and hit on everything that Barry had described and more.

Marlene felt an energy pushing back in the first-floor bedroom and got the name of this female spirit as Nadine, who is determined to take control. According to Marlene, Nadine did not like her telling us this. Nadine, whom Kate said was wearing a kerchief on her head, had been in the home a long time and deemed it her place. Marlene picked up the little ghost girl, said her name was Olivia and described her as the same age and look that Barry had mentioned. Marlene picked up that Nadine is Olivia's grandmother, and there was another spirit named Carolyn, who was an overbearing spirit, as she had been in life. She was Olivia's mother. It was an entire matriarchal spiritual line in one house.

We all went upstairs, and Marlene was drawn to the bedroom that Barry had previously stated he was afraid to be in. We walked into the bedroom, which was empty of all furnishings, with only a couple boxes in one corner. Marlene picked up negative energy right away, as well as multiple spirits. Bernadette walked into the closet and immediately picked something up with her psychic gifts. Marlene was also drawn to the closet and confirmed Bernadette's experience that there was something paranormal and significant. The closet was a portal from the other world where ghosts could walk into Barry's house. It was at this point that Marlene picked up the spirits of twin boys in the corner where Barry had always been afraid to go. These twin ghosts were cowering in the corner, confused about where they were and by the multitude of spirits traveling back and forth through the portal. Kate and Bernadette also picked up a negative energy in the room that would come back as a dark malignance later in the evening. In the light, this dark energy was toned down but would gain courage in the darkness. We all walked into the other bedroom on the second floor, with Bernadette and Marlene Marello both stating the room felt flat and spiritless. Barry confirmed that nothing has ever happened in that room.

We all headed down to the basement, and I felt that something was not right, as Barry's dog Bailey had followed us all over the house yet refused to go down into the basement. Instead, he stood at the top of the stairs and whined in fear. I've always been told that animals have senses beyond those of humans, much like how young children are more open to things than adults. My instincts proved correct when Marlene stated that the portal originated from the basement and worked straight up to the closet on the second floor and that the basement was filled with negative energy. She felt this negative energy was in the home when it was a brick-making place. The Shack had been haunted since its beginnings.

The equipment for the night included four digital night-vision video cameras that would be wired into the four-way monitor in the minivan in the driveway. We would also have hand-held digital recorders, Gauss and K2 meters for measuring disturbances, the spirit box and digital cameras. When we did the sweep of the house, my Gauss meter and Kate's K2 failed to register anything at all, yet when I went back up to the haunted bedroom on the second floor, I stood in the middle of the room to write something down on my notepad and the meter pegged all the way to red. I also stood in front of the home when the psychic sweep first began and snapped a photo that shows large orbs there, as if they knew what was coming and were responding.

The newest piece of equipment was a "grid" device that would show a red square grid pattern on the floor and walls so if anything unseen walked through it, we would detect the movement. This was set up in the second-floor bedroom. The night-vision digital cameras were set up in the basement, the first-floor bedroom, the back room off the kitchen and the second floor, where the portal was. The group also had trigger objects. Barry had found in the basement a very old shoe for a little girl. Marlene confirmed it was Olivia's. We also had a silver spoon that Barry had found wrapped in cheesecloth and stuffed into the wall when he was remodeling and tearing down the wall. Marlene did a reading on the spoon and determined it had been used in a ritual to ward off an illness. It had been dipped in a substance, wrapped and ceremonially placed in the wall, which was not an uncommon practice in the nineteenth century. We also had an old pissing pot that Barry found in the basement. This was from middle-of-the-night bathroom trips back in the days when people had outhouses and there was no indoor plumbing.

It was past 9:00 p.m., and the first team to go into the home was David, Ed, Josh and Marlene. Barry stayed in his kitchen. The rest of the group went outside and sat in the van where we could watch the four-way monitor and note any recorded activity. Mike had the notebook on his lap in the van and would write down the camera number and time of any occurrences. We witnessed many orbs while sitting in the van, but one was rather large and

Spirit lights and the dead roam through the portal inside the attic at the Shack.

pulsating and had a dark hole in the center. Otherwise, we chatted while watching the group members go from room to room for the next hour. We did observe Barry's cat strolling into the second-floor room all by itself and staring at the wall next to the portal. It seemed rather odd, yet cats are naturally curious little critters.

When the group was finished with its investigation, we went into the house to get a rundown on what the team experienced. Marlene said that when the group was upstairs by the portal, she was pushed by Nadine, the spirit that did not want us in the house. It was in this same room that Josh had felt the little girl ghost Olivia, who was following them from room to room during their investigation. Also, near the portal, David reported seeing a shadow person go across the room and went from being down low toward the floor to going up high by the ceiling. It was during the investigation that Barry, who sat in his kitchen with Bailey, heard constant whispering and spiritual chattering. This could not have come from the team members, who barely spoke and were upstairs or in the basement. Barry also was freezing cold, bundled up with a heavy sweatshirt and shivering, although the room was very warm. I was excited to be involved with the second team that was composed of Bernadette, Kate, Mike, Barry and myself. Barry had decided to come along with us on this part of the investigation, although Bailey would be left in the kitchen and was not too happy about that. He stayed by the door and wailed for his friend and master. We brought along the trigger object to see if we could get a response. We went to Barry's first-floor bedroom first and didn't get anything in there, but Bernadette spotted an entity standing in the corner of the adjacent living room. She took a small step forward and asked, "Who are you? Why are you here?" There was no audible response, but sometimes we can pick up the answers on the digital recorders. I had one in my hand and was standing right near the area.

We moved up to the second-floor bedroom near the portal, and something would happen that would trigger the most emotional paranormal encounter I have ever witnessed. As soon as we got into the bedroom, Bernadette sensed there was an entity in the room with us. We all did an EVP session when Kate felt compelled to go into the attic. The entrance to the attic was a small door in the bedroom that you had to bend over to go through. It was a small room that had a chimney coming through it and old boards nailed down that you could walk on. Marlene asked Barry if he would like to come into the room, so he followed. He was holding the pissing pot that had the other trigger objects inside of it: the spoon and Olivia's shoe. I walked in behind them with the digital recorder. Bernadette and Mike decided to stay in the bedroom. We were inside the attic when Barry said he felt compelled to go to the back corner where there was a small window. Marlene and I followed him, and he halted short of the area and just stood there frozen in fear. Even though it was dark, I could still make him out, for Marlene and I were close. It was at this point that I could hear Bernadette in the other room stating a ghost shadow figure had just walked past her and Mike and was heading in our direction. Within seconds of Bernadette's witnessing of this entity, Barry stated there was something standing in the corner of the attic looking at us. I heard a slight rattle and looked over at Barry, who was in such terror that his hands were shaking. The trigger objects were rattling around inside the pissing pot. Kate Geary sensed his fear and tried to calm him with her soothing voice. "You OK, Barry?" she asked gently. "I'm having trouble breathing. I have to get out of here," he said as he whisked right past me and back out the small door into the second-floor bedroom and into the hall, where he stood against the wall and broke down crying. Bernadette quickly threw her arms around him and reassured him that everything was OK. This was his home, and these spirits were guests. He had the power. Kate came over and was reassuring him, as was Mike, and I stood back speechless. I didn't get the feeling the ghosts were evil or malicious, just intruding spirits that were overwhelming their host. We all walked Barry back downstairs and into his kitchen as he didn't want to continue. We didn't go back to the investigation for a few minutes while Bernadette and Kate calmed him down and reassured him he was doing nothing wrong.

We resumed our investigation by going down into the basement. The walls were constructed of thin rocks layered on top of one another with cement in between. We conducted an EVP session, and Kate and I went into the little root cellar room and asked questions. David called us via our walkie-talkies and said there was a ton of orb activity once we came down into the cellar.

We went back upstairs and met back up with the rest of the group in the kitchen. It was now 10:30 p.m., and the next group to investigate would be Bernadette, David, Josh and Ed. It was during this next investigation while in the attic that Josh stated he was warming up. The attic is unheated, but this encounter with the ghost kiln confirmed one of Barry's previous experiences.

The highlight of the paranormal experience was at the end of the evening when Bernadette made the decision to have Marlene cleanse the entire house in a psychic ritual that I had never seen before. Since this was Barry's home, he was asked and agreed to be an active participant. Marlene filled a bowl with water and placed salt in it, and the entire group went up into the second-floor bedroom where Barry had his frightful encounter and where the portal was located. Mike Geary had the spirit box running. Everyone sat on the floor in a circle, and Bernadette began an EVP session. Kate placed a flashlight in the center of the circle in the dark room, and when questions were being asked, she requested the spirits to turn on the flashlight. Within seconds, there was a response, and the small flashlight lit up. It was during this session that Bernadette saw a dark shadow figure bent over in a grotesque shape at an almost unholy angle. Right after this, Marlene picked up the spirit by the name of Robert, which had been the malignant ghost Bernadette had just witnessed. He communicated with the psychic that he was here because of the portal and couldn't get back through the spirits that were blocking his way, so Marlene and Barry went into the attic and started to both dip their hands into the salt water and spritz it about, repeating, "All negativity, all negative energies leave." Marlene explained to the ghost Robert to follow her back to the portal. The entire group chanted in unison, "All negativity, all negative energies leave" over and over again until Marlene and Barry cleansed all the way into the closet where the portal was located.

The rest of the house was ritualized with the same spiritual cleansing. The evening investigation had concluded, and everyone had gathered in the kitchen. David, Ed, Gary and Josh started to pick up all the equipment and cords. I was in the hallway next to the kitchen and was looking over the digital photographs I had taken when I heard a metal clicking noise and looked up to the door that was five feet in front of me. I witnessed the doorknob turning, the door clicking open and then swinging all the way open until it banged against the wall. I thought one of the team members was in this room—until I took a few steps and realized that there was nobody in there. "Oh, my God!" I exclaimed and immediately went into the room where Bernadette was standing and told her what happened. I had never had anything like this happen to me, never in my entire life, never on any ghost investigation. There were no windows in the room, and there was no vent blowing air. Besides, the doorknob turned and clicked, and then the door opened all the way as if a ghost had walked through it.

The night concluded with a closing prayer where we held hands and Bernadette prayed that all positive energies remain and that we would all be protected in the name of the Lord. The last thing Kate, Marlene and Bernadette did was give Barry a hug and reassure him that everything would be OK and to call them if he had any more occurrences. My last sight was of Barry, his dog Bailey and his cat all huddled together in the kitchen, content. It was an emotional night for the entire team and one I doubt would ever be repeated.

Additional Observations from Bernadette Peck

I knew right away the Shack was going to be an incredibly active investigation based on the pre-investigation sweep. I brought with me Marlene Marello, a psychic, and we discovered dark energy right away and one female entity that was hostile toward Marlene. During the investigation, we picked up the names of spirits, including a woman named Nadine; a little girl named Olivia; Anna, the protector of the owner; and Robert. These spirits were active the night of the investigation, and spikes occurred all over the place, including the ghost Nadine pushing Marlene multiple times and telling her to leave. Josh had a paranormal hot flash in the kitchen that was overwhelming in its intensity, while David heard and picked up a growl and I witnessed a shadow person in a second-floor bedroom. Marlene discovered that the closet in this room was a portal, and she closed the door and did her best to cleanse the house. Barry broke down with emotion, and Marlene and I comforted him. At the close of the investigation, he felt better. I followed up weeks later, and Barry said he felt much better and that there was still something there, but it was friendly. He sent me a photo he took of the face of a female spirit looking at him in his bedroom. I was pleased we had rid the Shack of the angry and negative and left behind the light and friendly. To this day, the Shack is serene.

Chapter 12

VERNON PUBLIC LIBRARY

Vernon, New York—Saturday, October 13, 2012

The Vernon Public Library is a quaint little structure a stone's throw from Route 5 in Vernon, New York, that once had a visit from prolific writer and pop icon Stephen King. The library is ground zero as the weekly meeting site for the Ghost Seekers of Central New York and at one time was host to horses as a carriage house. Who knew that a tiny two-story place of learning and books would host lively and engaging spirits and restless ghosts? The Ghost Seekers of Central New York arrived at the library at eight in the evening and included lead investigator Bernadette Peck, David Peck, Len Bragg, Carol Pearo, Helen Clausen and yours truly. We were greeted by Rob and Gary Seelman, who are always working the counter and obviously love the little library with all their hearts. It was Rob who told the group of his time in the library as a little boy when his mother worked the counter. He had a paranormal experience when books flew off a shelf that was clear on the other side of the library. He also told the group of the spot in the reading room corner that is always cold and the footsteps they could hear on the second floor when there was nobody else in the library.

We were intrigued, but our team had never investigated such a small structure and had to figure out the best place to host ghost central. There was a small storage room right behind the front desk, so Rob and a couple of the Ghost Seekers cleared enough of the clutter and books out of the way to be able to place the monitor where we could be segregated from the team that would be starting the investigation. After a walk-through, it was decided to place a couple cameras on the second floor, where Bernadette had located an old display case that had an assortment of old medical equipment, journals and pictures. The second floor had once been rented to a doctor who practiced from the location. The area seemed to give off a spooky vibe, so everyone agreed with Bernadette's feelings. She determined the best place for the cameras would be on the first floor looking over the bookshelves and the stairs to the second floor. We also placed one camera overlooking the display case of the medical items.

Team one was Carol, Helen and Bernadette. They went upstairs and performed an EVP session while I stayed back in ghost central with Len and David. We watched the monitors closely, and we had a spiral notebook there in case we witnessed something. We log experiences so it is easier to go back through the evidence. We noticed a few small orbs and logged them. Within an hour, the ladies returned, so we decided to take a break and sit out in the reading room to discuss a few things before team two was to take to the upstairs. It was at this point that Helen started to get an odd feeling. The corner of the room where she was sitting had been one of the spots where Rob and Gary had experienced cold spells. Helen was getting frigid, so Len

The Vernon Public Library, the nerve center and meeting location of the Ghost Seekers of Central New York.

aimed the temperature gauge at the area. It was revealed that it was much colder than the rest of the room. This spot would come into play later in the evening with our fearless leader Bernadette.

Team two was David, Len and I. We climbed the stairs to the second floor, which was filled with stacks of books and chairs that we had to slalom through to get to the back room where the medical office used to be. It was in this area that we experienced a paranormal interaction that never disappoints: knocking. David and Len were asking questions, and we were getting light taps on the wood floor in response. After this, we also heard what we thought were voices on the stairwell coming up to the second floor. The ladies were in ghost central, all quiet, so we knew it was talking from the other side, from the spiritual zone, breaking through the wall of our fleshy dimension. We couldn't make out the words, as it sounded like mumbles, but it was definite talking.

We came back downstairs, and we were all excited at how the investigation was going. We decided to all sit as a group in the reading room, with Bernadette sitting in the corner where Helen had experienced her interaction earlier that evening. The same cold feeling came back, but this time physical contact was made. I was sitting right next to Bernadette when a spiritual ghostly hand touched her neck and hair. I have been on dozens of investigations, and Bernadette is always calm, cool and professional. I'd never seen her like this. It was not an evil or malignant dark energy touch but rather one of almost love and gentleness. It excited Bernadette and the rest of the group.

This was now a second strong paranormal interaction at the same spot. Within minutes of this happening, we had further strong evidence of the afterlife when we all heard what sounded like something bumping into our night-vision camera tripod. The entire group was in the next room, and there was nobody within twenty feet of the tripod. When we went back and reviewed the footage, it was startling. Indeed, the camera moved on the tripod as if it were bumped or pushed, yet there was absolutely nothing near it. When you get a strong piece of paranormal evidence, it makes the heart race. It validates all the hard work and research the group puts into these investigations—and perhaps it proves that we don't disappear when we die. Our spirits go on. Our life energy coexists with mortals of the living realm. Our souls persevere.

The night ended with the group standing together, holding hands, performing our closing prayer. In case you are wondering why the Ghost Seekers of Central New York perform such a ritual, it's simple. We embrace the good and discourage the evil. We wish to bring forth spirits of the pure and discourage the stained. We do not want to pursue demonology, nor do we want to have dark entities attaching themselves to us where we could bring these evil parasites back to our individual homes.

ADDITIONAL OBSERVATIONS FROM BERNADETTE PECK

This investigation was near and dear to my heart since this is the nerve center where the Ghost Seekers of Central New York meet. Long had we heard of the spirits in the cute little stone building, and we were not disappointed. Physical contact caught on camera is always exciting, and the spirits smacked into our night-vision camera sitting on the tripod. Half the team was in ghost central and the other half upstairs when the downstairs camera moved from a ghost bumping it or attempting to push it over. We had a steady stream of spirit energy on camera two, which was pointed at the corner of the reading room. It was the exact spot where Helen was sitting when she felt frozen. The rest of the team was sitting in proximity and experienced the same cold feelings. Then we all felt a presence in this area, along with hearing creepy whispering. The second floor had some great ghostly interactions with Len hearing knocking, Helen getting a cold spiritual rub while sitting in a chair and throaty sounds right behind a group of investigators. When we asked, "Do you want us to stay?" we received back a double knock. Dennis had a great EVP on his digital recorder: when asked if the spirit was Bieta Lewis, the name of a deceased person given to us by the employees of the library, a loud moan was heard.

Chapter 13

DURHAMVILLE FIREHOUSE

Durhamville, New York—Saturday, December 8, 2012

Durhamville is one of those one-stoplight towns that is populated by decent, hardworking Americans, the hearty stock of people who helped to build this great nation. It was in the heart of this town that the Ghost Seekers of Central New York would conduct an investigation at a place of reverence in any small town: the firehouse.

I drove out into the approaching dark, blotchy night that was damp and dreary, the kind of night that makes one want to curl up in front of a fireplace with a good book and a cup of hot cocoa. The firehouse was right in the main part of town, a two-story structure that supposedly hosted paranormal events. Volunteer firefighters are not the type of people for exaggeration or nonsense. They put their lives on the line to protect their fellow townspeople and make absolutely zero money to do so. These brave men and women of Durhamville had been experiencing ghostly interactions in their house of the brave.

I arrived a half hour early, and Bernadette and David Peck were already waiting in the parking lot sipping their coffee, waiting for the rest of the group to arrive. It didn't take long for Len and Helen to pull into the parking lot, so we headed into the firehouse to meet with the chief and the others. Alan Smith, fire chief, and his wife, Debbie, welcomed us and escorted us to the first-floor office so they could give us a rundown on the haunted happenings. The first thing they talked about was the bar/restaurant that used to be in what was now the fire station parking lot. They thought the

The Durhamville Firehouse.

name of the establishment was Ma & Pa's, and apparently there had been a fight and a murder in the place. They did know that when the place was demolished, the rubble was not taken away but rather was pushed into the cellar and dirt was paved over the top. This could be the cause of some of the haunting of the fire station since the structure was built on the parking lot of the old restaurant.

It was brought to our attention that another ghost group had done an investigation of the Durhamville Fire Station and had come up with the name of Sally as a possible entity walking the building. Alan and Debbie claimed that Ma & Pa's had a waitress named Sally who not only worked in the building but also lived upstairs. There was no way to verify this or the rumor that Sally provided "desserts" upstairs to male patrons. Alan and Debbie also mentioned that a long time ago, there had been a drowning in the Erie Canal, which runs right behind the firehouse. All these tragedies could certainly explain the paranormal instances. This is when the Ghost Seekers started to get the details of what was happening at the fire station and why they reached out for our help. Debbie said she gets the feeling you're being watched, especially out on the dining hall area of the fire station. Debbie and her group were using the ghost app on their smartphones and were able to glean some feedback.

We don't deny something paranormal was happening at the firehouse, as there were things like sightings of shadow people and crashing sounds out near the trucks where nothing could be found to have fallen, but the best recurring evidence was the turning of the gambling wheel. In the back of the firehouse, there is a small storage room with a large fuel tank that is named the "oil room." Stored against the back wall is a spinning wheel that the firefighters use on gambling night to raise money. Although the wheel was sitting down and not able to move, the firefighters kept hearing the clinking of the wheel turning. They would rush to the room, but there would be nothing in there, and the wheel would not be moving.

We decided to do our walk-through with Alan and Debbie so they could point out the paranormal hot spots and we could place the night-vision cameras there to see if we could get any otherworldly evidence. It was when we were up on the second floor, in the commissioner's room that was now host to some exercise equipment, that Bernadette got an ill feeling in the pit of her stomach. Pointing out the storage closet down the hall, Debbie told us of a fireman's helmet that came off the hook and fell to the floor. Upon inspection, we felt it could have been a paranormal experience, for the hook was not the type that the helmet could just fall off, and it certainly couldn't fall from someone walking by or even hitting the wall. The helmet was very secure on the hook and had to be carefully pulled up and around. The locations for the cameras were chosen, and when I was in the exercise/commissioner's room, I found a small gambling wheel that had been constructed out of the front rim and forks of a bicycle. This was a smaller version of the large gambling wheel heard by the firefighters. I set it on the bench of the exercise equipment in case any entity decided to give it a spin. We all gathered back into the office, and before we did our protection prayer, I noticed a framed copy of the Fireman's Prayer, which stated:

When I am called to duty, God,
wherever flames may rage,
Give me strength to save some life
Whatever be its age.
Help me embrace a little child
Before it is too late.
Or save an older person
From the horror of that fate.
And hear the weakest shout,
And quickly and effectively

To put the fire out.
I want to fill my calling
And to give the best in me,
To guard my every neighbor,
And protect his property.
And if according to your will
I have to lose my life,
Please bless with your protecting hand,
My children and my wife.
Amen.

I was thankful to read such brave words dedicated to the people who would give their lives to save others. We gathered and held hands in prayer, with Debbie joining in. Bernadette always leads us in prayer and eases the fears of the gathered before the ghost hunting was to begin. Team one would be Bernadette, Len and Helen. David and I would stay back in ghost central, where Debbie and Alan would sit with us and quietly watch as we would scribe in the spiral notebook anything seen by the night-vision cameras. It's amazing to watch a pitch-black room via these cameras, for things are captured that the naked eye cannot see. We watched as Bernadette and company went right up to the second floor and the room that she had the bad feelings about. There was about a ten-minute flurry of orbs that started as soon as team one settled in and started its EVP session. Debbie and Alan could easily tell the difference between dust floating and actual pulsating balls of paranormal energy, and the firehouse had them in abundance. When the ten minutes were up, the orbs and activity suddenly ended.

Later, Bernadette stated that the group had seen a shadow figure outside the room and going down the hall that coincided with the activity caught on the night-vision cameras. Carol arrived a little late but just in time to go with David and I as team two would go out into the dining hall where volunteers had seen a shadow person wandering in the far back corner. We sat at the back table, and David shot the session on his hand-held digital video camera while I snapped digital pictures with Bernadette's camera. Within a minute, it looked like I captured a nice orb by the Christmas tree while Carol was using the Gauss meter that also had a temperature measurement on it. She felt cold, and the temperature in her area moved from fifty-nine to sixty-three degrees within seconds while the Gauss meter spiked up to 3. In our sweep, there was nothing in the area where Carol was sitting, so we knew we had something paranormal in the vicinity.

When the activity died down, we went out to walk around the trucks. It was obvious that something was following Carol, for as we walked between the fire trucks, the Gauss meter kept spiking, and the temperature kept fluctuating. David took out his flashlight and turned it off. We asked questions and encouraged the spirits to pour their energy into the device and illuminate it. We had tried this earlier with no success, but this time when David asked anybody present to please light up the flashlight, the beam came on bright and clear.

Our next stop was the oil room where the large gambling wheel was located. We did not get anything to spin it, but David heard footsteps on the second floor as if something were walking right over the top of us. We all stopped talking, and it was so quiet you could hear yourself breathe when it happened again, footsteps of the dead. We looked at each other in astonishment; there was nobody upstairs, as the rest of the group was sequestered in ghost central.

The biggest fright of the night occurred as we were walking back to where the others were. Carol said that the kitchen made her feel creepy. At this point, I took a digital photo, and it looked like a black mass was looming over her head. Then I took another picture of Carol, and an image of a malignant malicious face appeared on the background on the door that was right behind her. Both pictures were unexplainable and unable to be debunked. Try as we could, we could not replicate either image. The dark energy threw the normally rock-solid David and Bernadette, with Helen and Len exchanging serious glances and explaining that they knew what it was and had encountered this type of dark energy in previous investigations. This is why we open and close with a prayer to ward off the dark and keep the evil at bay.

It was time to close everything down, so I asked Len and David if they wanted to go upstairs and do a five-minute EVP session, as I had not gone up there during the investigation. The far room on the second floor seemed flat, so we went to the storage area where the helmet had been reported to have flown off the hook. It was here that David had a hot encounter—heat of the paranormal kind. He stepped back from the room and stated that his legs, from the knees down, were flaming hot. It was interesting that he would have that kind of other-dimensional experience within the confines of a house dedicated to the extinguishing of flames.

The best EVP of the night was about to happen, and like all these ghostly encounters, it happened when you least expect it or look for it. We went into the room with the exercise equipment, and the first thing I said was,

"It would be nice if somebody would play with this wheel." I was referring to the small gambling wheel I had set on the exercise bench in hopes that a ghost would give it a whirl. Well, Len and David were on the other side of the room, so I was the closest to the wheel, and I was at least four feet away from it. We were settling in when all of the sudden, I heard a twang, as if something reached out and plucked one of the spokes on the wheel. I was shocked that it had happened and asked Len if he had bumped into anything. He said no, and David hadn't moved. I was in shock and thought maybe I was hearing things. Later, I listened to my hand-held digital recorder; there it was, clear as could be. It was the most amazing EVP, and the experiences and sounds heard by the firefighters had been verified within the last ten seconds of the investigation. We gathered and said our closing prayer, and I took one last look at the Durhamville Firehouse. It certainly lived up to its haunted reputation.

ADDITIONAL OBSERVATIONS FROM BERNADETTE PECK

The level of ghostly activity at the Durhamville Firehouse would be described as "fire-engine red" or of a "hot" level. Durhamville is a small town that is a wonderful slice of bygone America, and the quaint volunteer fire department is the nerve center.

The station yielded wonderful results of the paranormal. I could feel the spirits before I walked in the door. I felt as if I was being watched, and a voice said "hungry." We took a bunch of digital photos, and one caused great debate among the investigators, as it looked like an evil face on the door. We had streaks of paranormal ectoplasm light, orb activity and a flashlight response of an intelligent kind as questions were asked. Our paranormal query was answered, with every investigator on the team getting ghost interaction. Carol witnessed a shadow figure bolting across the engine room. Len's recorder picked up a spirit voice saying, "It's chilly in here." Dennis and Len recorded and witnessed the gambling wheel moving and the "ting" of the spokes as a ghost hand spun the wheel. Helen verified this as she was near the wheel when it was moved. I saw a shadow figure moving by the kitchen door. The reports of paranormal activity were verified in the evening, including the spirits walking about, the noises and the spinning of the firefighter's gambling wheel. There is no doubt that the ghosts speak to the living around the Durhamville Firehouse.

SOURCES

Dudajek, David. "A True Story or a Ghost Story." *Utica (NY) Observer Dispatch*, October 31, 1988.

Forest Hill Cemetery. www.foresthillcemetery.org.

Harf, Mark. "Utica State Hospital." Historic Asylums. www.rootsweb. ancestry.com/~asylums/utica_ny.com.

Henry Hiteman Engine & Hose Company, West Winfield Fire Department. http://westwinfieldfd.com.

Hudson, Cally. *A Short History of the First Presbyterian Church*. N.p.: self-published by members of the First Presbyterian Church, 1993.

LaDuca, Rocco. "Did the Devil Make Them Do It?" *Utica (NY) Observer Dispatch*, March 9, 2010.

Landmark Society of Greater Utica. "Rutger-Stueben Park Historic District and Rutger Park." www.uticalandmarks.org.

Madison House. www.themadison-house.com.

Magill, Martha. "Masters and Wardens of Newport Lodge #445, F. & A.M. 1885 to 2001." http://herkimer.nygenweb.net.

Native Languages of the Americas Online Resources. "Legendary Native American Figures: Oniate (Dry Fingers, Dry Hand, Oniata)." www.native-languages.org/morelegends/oniate.htm.

Parrotta, Lou, and Scott Fiesthumel. *Forest Hill Cemetery*. Utica, NY: Erie Canal Publications, 2012.

Players of Utica. "Our History." www.playersofutica.org.

Stanley Center for the Arts. "History." www.thestanley.org.

St. Volodymyr Great Ukrainian Catholic Church History. Jersey City, NJ: self-published by the members of the church, 1978.

Utica Daily Press. "Utica's Fine Homes." February 21, 1966.

Utica (NY) Saturday Globe. "A Brilliant Wedding at Westminster Church and in the MacKinnon Mansion." June 18, 1910.

Wikipedia. "Masonic Temple, Newport Lodge #445 Free & Accepted Masons." http://wikipedia.org/wiki/Masonic_Temple_%E2%80%94_Newport_Lodge_No._445_F.&A.M.

ABOUT THE AUTHORS

Dennis Webster is a paranormal investigator with the Ghost Seekers of Central New York. His previous works include *Haunted Mohawk Valley*, *Wicked Adirondacks*, *Wicked Mohawk Valley*, *Klock*, *Adirondack Mysteries* Volumes 1 and 2 and *Daisy Daring & the Quest for the Loomis Gang Gold*. He has a bachelor's of science degree from Utica College and a master's of business administration (MBA) from the State University of New York Institute of Technology (SUNYIT) in Utica/Rome. He lives in the beauty of the Mohawk Valley of central New York. He can be reached at denniswbstr@gmail.com.

Bernadette Peck, founder and lead investigator of the Ghost Seekers of Central New York, lives in Vernon, New York. For fifteen years now, she has been researching and investigating ghosts, which has led her to a very profound view of life after death and the knowledge that comes with the spiritual side of life.